Dearest jus Ellie,

CLIMB UP
WAY UP HIGH

*God Loves you.
and so do I.*

Esther B. Jimenez

CLIMB UP WAY UP HIGH

The Way to survive any trials in life is to struggle going up until the struggles are left down to serve as stepping stones.

ESTHER B. JIMENEZ

Climb Up Way Up High

Copyright © 2020 by Esther B. Jimenez. All rights reserved.

No part of this publication may be reproduced, stored in a retrieval system or transmitted in any way by any means, electronic, mechanical, photocopy, recording or otherwise without the prior permission of the author except as provided by USA copyright law.

The opinions expressed by the author are not necessarily those of URLink Print and Media.

1603 Capitol Ave., Suite 310 Cheyenne, Wyoming USA 82001
1-888-980-6523 | admin@urlinkpublishing.com

URLink Print and Media is committed to excellence in the publishing industry.

Book design copyright © 2020 by Esther B. Jimenez. All rights reserved.

Cover Design and Illustrations by Esther B. Jimenez

Published in the United States of America

Library of Congress Control Number: 2020903117
ISBN 978-1-64753-227-7 (Paperback)
ISBN 978-1-64753-228-4 (Digital)

14.02.20

CONTENTS

Dedication 7
Prologue 9
Preface 13
Introduction 17
Acknowledgements 21
About The Author 23
Foreword 25
Feedback (From A Millennial Point Of View) 27

CHAPTER

Who Am I? 29
Depersonalization 33
Anxiety 36
Depression 39
Plight To Fight 43
Welcome To America 47
Kill The Time 51
Back To Usa 55
Discovery 59
Steps To Recovery 62
Share-Share A Ride 67
Mental Health Counseling 70
Keep Going 73
I Am A Climber 75
The Outcome Is Rewarding 78

The Alphabet Of Esther 80
Self-Analysis 83
Life Goes On 86
Total Shift 90
Psychological Pain 93
Disability 96
Blessed Are The Handicaps 99
Suicidal Thoughts 102
Psychodynamics 105
Support Of The Family And Friends 112
The Final Curtain 115
The Beauty Of Words 117
I Witness From My Heart 122
D.A.D. Challenge
(Depersonalization, Anxiety And Depression) 129
Good News 131

Epilogue 133

DEDICATION

TO MYSELF, for I AM CREATED IN GOD'S IMAGE

To my (Late Parents) Honorata B. Jimenez and Pedro T. Jimenez.

To my brothers, my sister, my in-laws, my nephews, my nieces, and my grandchildren.

To my Best Friend, (You know who you are).

To All Victims of D.A.D. (Depersonalization, Anxiety and Depression) and the Depression Survivors.

To my Psychiatrist and Psychologist.

To All Mental Health Counselors, Psychiatric Nurses and Social Workers.

PROLOGUE

There is an immediate remedy for any discomfort. Analgesic or pain pill for headache, an antibiotic for infection and splint support for simple fracture.

For mental pain, what can we take? What can we have? Are we aware of mental health? How about mental illness?

It so happened that this month of May is the month of Mental Health Awareness.

It is significant on my part because I started writing my manuscript few days ago, unaware that this month is a Mental Health Awareness month. The book I am writing is about Depression. My name is Esther B. Jimenez, I am a Depression Survivor. Mental Health is just as important as physical health and tantamount to say, should be given attention, as to the education and awareness of mental illness existence. This month, is also awareness of triumph of the human spirit. Confession publicly or coming out is a sign of victory and the real triumph of the human spirit. It is a relief, a concept of releasing the burden from the ***stigmatization***. And yes, *"**stigma attached**"* hinders the chance of mental health awareness. I came out from the ***stigmatization***. I came out from the world of Depression Denial.

The key to the success of mental wellness is to sincerely acknowledge that the depression is ***treatable***. I am acknowledging that I have history of depression. I had acknowledged that I was suffering from depression. I didn't think of what the people would say about me. I didn't even pay attention of the ***stigmatization***.

The worst thing that a victim of depression experienced is, the feeling of "no where to go like a confused, poisoned rat." As I go along sharing about my history of depression, you will find out more about my journey from the drowning to the surviving moments. So join me in this pathway, to prove to mankind that depression is ***treatable.*** I am the living sample of a Depression Survivor (the real soul being.)

Now this is a public confession, yet the bottom line is how I survived from the uncertainties in my life, from my dim moments and from the agony of mental pain and aches. Instead of sharing right away, speaking of the issues randomly or confessing directly, allow me to offer you one fervent prayer. This prayer will be the start of losing the tightness feeling on my chest.

THE PRAYER OF THE HUNGRY SOUL
(A Prayer of a Depressed Being)

I crave for the consoling words from a High Spirited Soul
I thirst for the water from the Holy Quencher
I seek for the power of the inner healing
I clenched my fist from my aching pains
O LORD, the Father of Mercy look into
The heart of Your grieving child
I grieved for the loss of my identity
I long for Your touch and warm embrace
I surrender myself and my all
Please lift me up from the agony of sins
My hungry soul I give in
O LORD, my GOD, my plea, I beg of You
To listen and grant me the peace I need
Here, now and forever, Amen!

This is only the beginning of my climbing the mountain of survivors, so I will Climb Up Way Up High!

I will continue climbing up way up high to defeat this triple mental illness, the D.A.D. (Depersonalization, Anxiety and Depression) challenge. Since there are three major mental illnesses that engulf my being human, (the Depersonalization, Anxiety and Depression), I would like to call this acronym the D.A.D. Challenge. I would be using this acronym in this book from time to time. For me it is easier to relay my battle since my mental illness occurred chronologically as to which illness attacked me first. It was indeed D.A.D. (Depersonalization, Anxiety and Depression.)

PREFACE

Statistically, mental illness ranks high in percentage worldwide. Among the mental illnesses, depression and anxiety rank high. We see these two mental illnesses as buddies. Dealing with depression is simultaneously dealing with anxiety.

First of all, I didn't use any numbers and figures for statistics, because there are enough resources of information that are available as references about mental illness. One of the organizations that can give facts and percentage figures about mental illness is the (NAMI), National Alliance on Mental Illness.

Secondly, numbers changed every year, gender, age, environmental wise and other more factors. Since women suffer from hormonal changes behavior, they are more prone to suffer depression like the postpartum psychosis cases.

Older adults are more prone than young adults, because older ones encountered more stressful situations than the latter.

Statistic says something about figures and numbers, but I chose the science of using information about people. But I suggest that if you want accurate percentage just refer to the different books and pamphlets that would give information about the accurate occurrence of mental health and behavioral disorders.

But as far as the percentage is concerned I can surely attest that 100% of the information that you will read from this book is truthfully shared and honestly admitted that, "I am a Depression Survivor", a victim of anxiety disorder, suffered early onset of depersonalization and the author of this book.

I have been wanting to write a book about depression before my other books, but I was a little bit hesitant. *"Stigma attached"!* That is the hesitancy I am referring to. So, what changed my mind on pursuing to write a book about "depression"?

Again, according to the research there are lots of people suffering from depression **untreated**. Why? Victims themselves ignored it and probably in **denial**. Or maybe because of the **stigmatization**.

I just turned seventy years old in November of 2017. During the celebration, I was asked to share about myself in the program. The truth was when I was preparing my speech, it dawned on me about how I survived this awful mental illness called, "depression". So I included in my speech a piece about how I survived. After writing the rough draft I had the time to ponder more. In my mind and in my heart, I would like to extend my thoughts, my enthusiasm to share, and my self-less goal, not only in a piece or part of the speech but to a bigger scope. I was ready to tell the world that "depression" will no longer be stagnant. It is *treatable* and I am one of the living souls, indeed a living testimony of true survivor. So from the time of writing the speech and mentioning about the history of my depression, I started pondering on when I can start going into a larger scale of sharing. Since I was still working on the progress of my manuscript I had to wait a little bit more. It was the first week of May when I started jotting down about the important and significant facts about eliminating the "stigma attached". Then it was on May 24 when my book entitled "GATHER AROUND THE TABLE" was released on line. So my adrenalin started to pump for the next book, entitled, "CLIMB UP WAY UP HIGH".

The significant facts I mentioned earlier were about my unforgettable memories of depression, my plight, my struggle and how I climbed up to survive. Since it was still the month of May which is also the month of Mental Health Awareness, as well as Mental Illness it was a great timing. I was indeed more inspired that I can contribute to this awareness month. So join me to honor this month of May to celebrate the wellness of mental health. Let us also congratulate the (NAMI), National Alliance on Mental Illness for their utmost support and love and taking care of the peoples' behavioral and mental status.

News around the world are heard, reporting about the suicides caused by substance abuse such as alcohol, cocaine overdose or any chemical intake. The bottom line is, this is triggered by depression.

People who are suffering from depression verbalized about their feelings of helplessness, hopelessness, fatigue, sleeplessness, irritability and more, yet they are being ignored by many, especially the victims themselves. And because of the **stigma attached**, victims themselves avoid the issue of suffering with this dreadful illness.

I believed that these things need attention. And this is where I need to enter.

"My name is Estrella B. Jimenez", I am a Depression Survivor".

The people who are victims of depression have something in common. They feel lonely, sad, hopeless and helpless; they manifest sleepless nights, fatigue, irritability and many more unpleasant uncertainties and unidentified feelings.

They described their feelings being entrapped in the dungeon, feeling imprisoned and feeling there's no way out.

I am with them, feeling what they feel. I am one of them. But I did not fall into the deeper pit. I managed to get away from the dungeon imprisonment.

I climbed my way up high. Again, there goes the title of my Book, "CLIMB UP WAY UP HIGH". I would like to go to the opposite direction. Instead of going down the pit, I will go up, up high by climbing, facing the struggles, fighting the plight and overcoming the fears.

I would be open and honest enough to share every bit of what I can share in regards to this *"stigma"* and *"malign"* mental illness named, "Depression."

Depression is not like a sprouting plant that comes no where. It has an origin. So this book will tell you the story of surviving ESTHER. She climbs up way up high.

Yes, I have gone through an unforgettable life experience. Millions of us experienced million kinds of symptoms, almost same ones, but again it is one of a kind depression.

So, I expect you my dear readers to climb up higher with me. This is what we need to survive. We should keep looking up to see how we can climb up. So depression "Get out of my way"

INTRODUCTION

Since majority of the population all over the world knows what depression is, and has concept of how dreadful it is and the stigma attached in it, let us help the world by supporting the victims, through our acknowledgement that it is ***treatable***. Let us extend our love through our acceptance and understanding of what they are going through.

One of the measures I did was, journaling my feelings. Part of my journaling was writing poems. I have at least four poems that I extracted from my volume I of What's In My Heart? These poems pertain to my depression episodes. I will use one of them now and the three will follow as we go along in this climbing up way up high book. I always write on my journal pad everything, especially the unpleasant feelings I had. This poem "Depression" was exactly the feelings I felt.

"DEPRESSION"

What's in a person's mind? What's behind someone's thoughts?
What's depression? A feeling of hopelessness, helplessness,
Low moments? Lack of interest or no interest at all to live? Not motivated to work or even to talk
Isolation, withdrawn behavior, coping mechanisms poor
Crying spells with no reason at all, grooming unaware
Always negative in all aspects, are you one of them?
A depressed being? I know how it felt, I was once in their place
Reaching out I did, talked it out indeed
Seeking professional help,

A psychiatrist, a psychologist?
Strong family support I received, everyday I was journaling
My feelings, my anxieties, to release my nervous tension,
The sleepless nights and continuous nicotine puff
I wrote them in my security pad,
With all the fervent prayers, the faith, and the belief,
I thank GOD, the Almighty for the inner healing
And the chance for me to serve Him
My depression is a Blessing, enlightenment for my being
Alas! I am healed through GOD's grace and power!

This is just a synopsis of my depression history. I mentioned in my poem that depression is a Blessing and I can attest to that. I learned to fight the plight of depression. I acquired the means to climb up way up high. The game to play in this world of dim is "struggle" to get away from being totally doomed.

Climbing up has a positive insight for those who aim in going to the top. I have my own interpretation of the phrase "Climb Up" in relation to how I deal with my dim moments.

- * Climb up is to ask for help
- * Climb up is to find a solution
- * Climb up is to search for oneself
- * Climb up is to never stop finding measures to survive
- * Climb up is to be willing to accept support.
- * Climb up is to hold on to something to help us to be pulled up
- * Climb up is not only struggling to be on top, but utilizing the parallel help.

My climbing up way up high is just like learning to swim, so you won't get drowned. This is a parallel comparison. Depression is a serious matter to deal with, to talk about, and a must be given attention and not to be ignored.

I thank the Almighty GOD for His love, giving me a chance to be back to my normal kind of life,(stress-free, anxiety- free, tension-free and other things like freedom from uncertainties and freedom from unpleasant occurrences)

I climbed up way up high, that's why I am here now to let the world know that I am a Depression Survivor, to let the world know that I am happy, I am well and to let the world know that depression is **treatable.**

I haven't tried the actual rock climbing even the man-made or artificial rock for climbing. Recently, I just went for a physical therapy for my imbalance in walking and with a little bit gait problem. One of my physical therapists was into rock climbing. I asked some questions about rock climbing. According to her, there are two ways a climber used in rock climbing. One is through bouldering and the other is through belay. She explained that bouldering performed on small rock walls (the boulders) without the use of harness or ropes. And the belaying involves two individuals. There is a leader to give instructions to tackle more difficult sections.

In belaying, there is a partner performing a critical role on the ground, ready to catch a fall and handles the rope skillfully. *Belaying refers to a variety of technique climbers use to exert tension on a climbing rope so that a falling climber does not fall very far.*

CLIMB UP WAY UP HIGH is the name of my book. I was inspired by the idea of rock climbing, especially when I heard from someone who had experienced to climb up way up high (the struggles encountered, yet with amazing outcome and there was a feeling of self-fulfillment)

I would like to compare my struggles, my plights, and trials in rock climbing. I did try to face the trials, combat the struggle, by acknowledging my mental problems through reaching out to my loved ones and journaling my feelings. I had to do these measures myself, (that is without ropes and harnesses). That is what we called, "bouldering"

Analogically speaking, I started to climb up and I was glad to be able to step up. But I needed more support and I had them. I consulted a psychologist, and a psychiatrist. I had my parents, friends and relatives who supported me all the way. So they were my belays, ready to catch me when I was being attacked by D.A.D (Depersonalization Anxiety and Depression.)

ACKNOWLEDGEMENTS

I thank GOD Almighty for the inner healing that He granted me.

I thank Dr. Patrick O'Connell, my psychologist whom I visited initially.

I thank Dr. Panom Phoungcherchoo, who has been my psychiatrist for many years.

I thank my parents (both already deceased), for their utmost support during my moments of attack.

I thank my cousin (Elizabeth P. Criste) who witnessed my anxiety attack and pacified me until I totally calmed down.

I acknowledge the people who shared their experiences regarding their mental illnesses, especially the triple mental illness, as D.A.D. (depersonalization, anxiety and depression.)

I am thankful for my own faith of being a Catholic especially my devotion to our Blessed Mother Virgin Mary and my saying of rosary very often, that helps me in my inner healing.

I thank the different organizations/agencies, hospitals, clinics for supporting and accommodating the clients with behavioral problems.

I am thankful to Ms. Maria Cora Pura, my sister in CHRIST for writing the Foreword of this book, giving her precious moments to share her feedback.

I acknowledge Francis John Angelo A. Jimenez, my nephew for his heartfelt input/feedback regarding the whole scenario of the mental illness as a millennial point of view.

I also acknowledge all the mental health counselors, psychiatric nurses and the social workers who are actively involved in taking care of mentally challenged and mentally- ill clients in the hospitals and in the clinics.

I would like to acknowledge the commendable gesture of our government officials in the promulgation of the new Philippine Mental Health Law or Republic Act 11036. I am one happy recipient of the good news.

Last but not the least, I also would like to acknowledge the rock climbers, mountain climbers, even wall climbers (climbing on man-made wall), and even an ordinary tree climber like climbing the tallest tree, who serve as inspirations in reaching ones goal.

ABOUT THE AUTHOR

Estrella B. Jimenez, "aka" Esther or Thea is originally from Manila, Philippines, a retired nurse, a US Citizen and presently residing in Chicago, Illinois USA.

She worked as a Mental Health Counselor for three years in one of the Psychiatric hospitals in Chicago. She is a member of Author's Marketing Group, in Illinois.

She received the Editor's Choice Award in August, 2004 and January 2008 by International Society of Poets. The Books she has written are the following:

1. 365 Days Food For Thoughts
2. Bible Tidbits
3. What's In My Heart? Vol.I
4. What's In My Heart? Vol.II
5. 202 Turtle Haiku
6. Have Phun With Elefants
7. Deep Inner Thoughts
8. Gather Around The Table

She is working on a manuscript, "Hay! Naku Haiku", "Spoken Words,", "The Art on the Rock," "101 Parables For All Of Us" and "Reflection of Courage".

Esther is a pet lover as evidenced by having a dog named "Benjie" and few turtles, and with one favorite turtle named, "Pong". She is a member of Chicago Turtle Club, a non-profit organization.

Esther Jimenez

A member of Bereavement Ministry, used to be a Eucharistic Minister and a Lector in her parish church.

Whatever Esther does, she prays for the guidance of the Holy Spirit and always relies on His power. For her, the Holy Spirit is her Spiritual Director.

FOREWORD

I never thought that I would have this honor and privilege to be a part of a dear friend, Esther's life in sharing her valuable life as a writer, author, and poet. Reading her manuscript on "CLIMB UP WAY-UP HIGH" page after page, I was profoundly shocked and amazed of her openness, genuineness and humility in relating the experiences she went through in her life from childhood years to adulthood, because of her depression and anxiety-triggered by few traumatic episodes.

When people are faced with difficulties and trials in their life, they become very negative. They start hating themselves and others including GOD. In her situation she flooded herself with so much faith, and kept on loving Him even more. She trusted GOD's Holy Spirit to bring upon her the healing she needed.

Esther is a woman of faith, hope, peace, joy and grace. Without these gifts she received from the LORD, where would she be today? She chose to endure the climbing on the rocky road.

My admiration for Esther is profoundly at a high level, because of her boldness and courage on how she survived every detail of her pain and fear. She is truly a survivor because of her deep faith in the LORD, and as a result she is very inspired and empowered by the Spirit of GOD. He Has endowed Esther with a beautiful heart, soul and spirit. As a person she is filled with charm and inner beauty.

I am grateful to GOD for you are a dear friend to me and my husband. We will continue to pray for you and all the works you do. May GOD bless you.

May this book inspire many people so they can climb up with Esther to reach GOD's glory.

Maria Corazon Pura RN, BSN

MARIA CORAZON PURA RN, BSN

First, I would like to express my sincere thanks to the author of this beautiful book, a dear friend of mine Esther.

My name is Maria Corazon Pura. If you know a little bit of Spanish, my name has a beautiful translation to English, "Pure Heart of Mary". As I grew older, I started to be like our blessed Mother because Mary's heart is pure. Hopefully through prayers GOD will continue to keep this desire and live it.

I belong to a family of eight children and I am the oldest. My parents were poor and raised my siblings from farming. An aunt of mine became, my surrogate mother due to Mom's chronic illness of lung disease. She adopted me when I was only a few months old. My aunt persevered in sending me to Catholic school where I studied Journalism, and finished the Bachelor of Science in Journalism, but never worked as a journalist. But I was led to one of the best nursing schools at St Luke's School of Nursing.

After my graduation I married the man GOD Has given me, a precious gift from Him and his name is Ben Pura. GOD blessed us with a beautiful son, Raymond. We have three grown children, two sons and a daughter, eight grandchildren. All along in my married and family life, JESUS Has been abiding us.

My nursing career was predominantly in Mental Health or Psychiatry. I spent my life mostly working as a Psychiatric nurse at Loyola University Medical Center for many years. I met Esther at a private psychiatric hospital where we worked together and we started our acquaintanceship then to a GOD given friendship. She was working as a Mental Health Counselor and I was working as a part time nurse. We helped each other and we learned from each other. It was indeed fun working with sister Esther. One thing I love about Esther is her faith, that had grown through the years and her love for the LORD grew stronger. She is a strong woman but remained humble. As am writing this, she and I have similar traits and gifts but the main blessing both of us have are: Faith and Love for the LORD eternally. I will remain your good friend in JESUS! Amen!

FEEDBACK
(From a Millennial Point Of View)
By FRANCIS ANGELO A. JIMENEZ

"Depression." This word has been thrown around easily among millennials. We use this to describe anything from a bad day to an overwhelming inability to live life. But for someone with depression, anxiety, and depersonalization, it is much more than any word can describe. That is why this book, a personal journey aims to help understand what it is like to undergo such struggles and overcome them.

My aunt's journey in life is very humbling. Not everyone has the strength to seek help, let alone tell the world about their mental health. But this is proof that life gets better. After reading this book, I felt my compassion towards others renewed. I felt that my empathy grew stronger. I felt the essence of being human. And I believe that anyone who reads this will understand these very same feelings. I cannot accurately describe what people with depression go through, but after discovering my aunt's story, it is enough for me to say that, in all honesty, it is unfair.

This is the book's purpose. While we all have different roads to walk in life, adventures to come upon, this is a certain story of a young "warrior girl" who grew up to be a fine warrior woman. We all have been assigned mountains to climb and she had hers. Perhaps, it takes a lifetime to even reach the peak. But we are fortunate because of the people we love like my aunt, who chose to tell her tale and show others that they can climb up, way up high.

Esther Jimenez

WHO AM I?

I have to be open and be honest if I will be thorough in relating my life in the midst of my dim moments. I was referring to my childhood life that was as early as seven years old. I was in my first grade in elementary school, when my curiosity was aroused. All of a sudden, I stood up from trying to sleep one night and I approached my father and asked him, "Who am I tatay?" Tatay is a Filipino word for father. It was not only a curious question, but my body was shaking and trembling when I asked him that. My voice did the same thing with trembling sound. I was also teary-eyed. There was a follow-up question like, "Am I going to die soon?" What a terrible question to ask, from a seven year old?

No one understood what went on after that. I was only seven years old and what do I know about those questions. I don't think it was a sign of being a genius child. But I remember vividly that my father used his two fingers, to spank me slightly on my left cheek. He did it to just shake me up or to wake me up in case I was just sleepy or I was just dreaming. It was an unforgettable moment in my life. The next day, I was feeling alright. This incident had something to do with my future! future! future! It didn't happen anymore during my continuous childhood life.

Then when I reached my young adulthood, that was before my internship in Nursing, my life also changed. I was supposed to go for my internship, but it didn't go through. I had an anxiety attack when I reached the nursing dormitory where I was going to be a nursing intern. I felt strange when the group of student nurses welcomed me. For some reason, I didn't feel comfortable. One of them was trying to be extra nice, and even told me in a very soft voice, "I like you." I asked myself, "What was that?" The more I was shaking and I didn't hesitate to leave the dormitory and never went back.

I stopped for one semester and my father got worried. He asked me if I want to seek for a professional help. I didn't hesitate at all. In other words we saw a psychiatrist.

By the way my father was working in a big government hospital as a mailman. He knew a lot of physicians and that included the psychiatrists. So we agreed for me to see a professional. This was my first visit to a psychiatrist.

I was diagnosed with Anxiety Disorder. The doctor prescribed me cod liver oil, a vitamin supplement because I was quite anemic then. I had at least few sessions, a once a week visit and had it for a period of one month. I tried to stay healthy for at least five to seven months. Then I was able to pursue my internship (not in the same hospital where I left before.) At last I graduated in Nursing the year 1970 at Marian College of Nursing, straight years with no back subjects.

But before our graduation there was another episode of anxiety attack. A month before graduation, we attended a weekend retreat. Right after the retreat I had an anxiety attack. I didn't know what to do. My classmates who were near me tried to help me. They wanted to take me to the hospital. But I told them I would be okay. It was a "struggle" indeed. I felt like a confused lamb running around without direction. I was so scared every time I looked at myself in the mirror. GOD knows I struggled every breath I took. I wasn't exaggerating. It was a zigzag road for me, with bumpy moments. Sometimes these bumpy moments were shaking my brain. And sometimes I liked it because the direction of my brain changed from confusion to just plain shaky. I liked it better rather than feeling empty headed. The second worst thing was a feeling of disconnection. I felt that my upper extremities (arms and hands) were not connected with my body. Totally, I lost my identity, not aware of who I was?

I am scared at the moment while I am relating it now. I am scared and nervous. Tension engulfs all over my body. But one thing funny was everytime I fixed my hair infront of the mirror I was rushing, fast forwarding my movements because I couldn't look at my face. Don't ask me why, because I didn't know. I would never forget the weird feelings I had. This was a scenario in my life that I could consider a blessing. While I was struggling, I was also searching for my true identity.

Though it was a terrible plight I didn't go to see my psychiatrist. I just started to be positive, going to the movies with friends. I read a lot of self-help books. I did some relaxation technique. I even went to the zoo by myself, with my pocket book to read. And I remember I read Bourne Identity by Robert Ludlum (my favorite). I read all his books that time. I had also a small notebook, my security pad to write on. I had a small radio called transistor with me. These help me in handling my uncertainties. This was the place I wrote my exploring poem entitled " MYSELF"

I went to the Manila Zoo from a night shift job at the hospital, to ponder on who I was. Yes, I was a bit depersonalized. I enjoyed watching the animals and seeing them eased up my confusion. They are indeed therapeutic. Here is MYSELF for you to read.

MYSELF

Do you know yourself? Just spare a moment
Analyze who you are, shall I do it too, to find out?
I am but myself, Nobody can deny
You are but yourself, who else can reply?
But is it enough to know, who you are or
Who I am?
Let's find out together,
Oh a lot of things to consider
To find out who am I?
Must I need to justify
Myself, my being, my image
I have to discover my true identity
Where are you myself?
I am here in the midst of discovery
Now I know the image I've grown

Esther Jimenez

> *Myself, I have found on my own*
> *I realized the truth behind myself*
> *That I am created in GOD's Image.*

So after more than four decades ago, there is a big change, I came to know myself. I have realized that I am created in GOD's Image, that GOD loves me and so do I. I learned to love myself.

DEPERSONALIZATION

When I first experienced the anxiety at the age of seven, no one had ever known. It remained that way, and it was only between me and myself.

Years gone by and I was still bugged by that dark shadow of uncertainties. Until the time I have encountered the "face to face" mirror incident. It was the time of my adulthood when I strongly felt this unexplainable encounter. I was looking at the mirror as if it was not me. When I looked at my arms and my hands it felt like they were disconnected from my body. I kept shaking my arms and my hands up and down to get rid of that feeling. For some reason, the feeling of weirdness was gone after few seconds.

I didn't know what was that feeling? Then occasionally it was visiting me. I never told such feeling to anyone. I kept it to myself. I didn't know that there was a term for that. It is "depersonalization". The first time I heard this word was when my psychiatrist mentioned it in one of our sessions. He didn't explain what depersonalization was. I have already mentioned such weird feelings in the chapter before this. I vividly described my feeling of uneasiness, with epigastric pain, and depersonalized as in detachment feeling.

Even at home if I was experiencing some kind of thought and disconnection feeling, I would just say, I am depersonalized again. It was easier for me to describe or to say, "I am depersonalized" rather than wandering what was I feeling. That word became my headache-like complaint.

It is more than we think. How about you? Have you ever felt disconnected from your own body? Or a numb feeling to anything?

Or looking at the mirror not recognizing yourself? If you do, you might be having a disorder like what I have, the "depersonalization".

The National Alliance on Mental Illness (NAMI) estimates that nearly 50% of all the adults in the United States experience depersonalization and at least once in their lives had either an isolated episode or a full blown disaster.

The NAMI mentioned at least six symptoms of depersonalization. Half of the numbers of symptoms were my own feelings. Clinically depersonalization can consist of a detachment within the self, regarding ones mind or body. A disorder is marked by periods of feeling disconnected or detached from ones body and thoughts. The disorder is sometimes described as feeling like you are observing yourself outside your body or like being in a dream. Depersonalization disorder is the feeling of being detached from ones feelings and body, from the environment, surrounding also termed as (derealization.)

Since I was a nurse I had an advantage of understanding the clinical aspect of depersonalization better and I can grasp easily because it pertains to my own diagnosis.

I didn't know before where this depersonalization came from? How did I get this? Why me? I have found out that the causes of depersonalization could be biological and environmental. Many dissociative disorders are triggered by experiencing intense stress or trauma, such as abuse, accidents, natural disasters or violence. So there are many contributing factors that cause "depersonalization".

In my case, I realized that I have an "identity crisis" and I know this is also a contributing factor. Growing-up I used to play boys' games. I am the oldest among the siblings in our family. I had a strong personality that sometimes mistaken as being boyish. I was a straight-forward too. I figured out that this is maybe one of the causes of my depersonalization resulting to identity crisis. But the beautiful thing that made me realized is the belief that I have GOD in my heart and because I was created in GOD's Image.

Just to think, I am created in GOD's Image is a powerful statement. It is just like a promisory note that will say, "I promise to stick with the Image I am created and I will be well." I won't go wrong as long as I have this beautiful Image of GOD in me. There is no medicine for depersonalization, but with fervent prayers, and with strong faith and with GOD's love, I know I would be able to survive and climb up high.

ANXIETY

I had no clue before, how this anxiety attacks a person. I have been anxious, jittery and very tensed, but I wasn't aware that they called it, "anxiety". I thought anxiety was just a plain palpitation, and fast pulse rate. Most especially I thought it was an acute one and a one time episode, but no, it turned out that it is a chronic one.

Anxiety is not just an attack like sneezing or coughing. It's more than that. After few attacks that I have experienced, I would prefer to have a toothache. In toothache there is certainty of pain experience. Anxiety is feeling of uncertainties and sometimes I feel like bumping my head on the wall. Why? If I bump my head and hit the wall, for sure I will feel the pain. And that was indeed a certainty.

One of the symptoms of Depression is anxiety. I have a poem written when I was having an attack of anxiety. In this poem I was expressing what I had experienced.

ANXIETY

Who can define anxiety except the guilty party?
Have you ever been victim of panic attack anxiety?
If so, you would know how it is to feel the uncertainty
There is this shaking inside, vacuum-air inside my
Skull, tight sensation of my brain,
The eyes teary and frightened, pacing back and forth
Stomach surrounded by butterflies
Washroom frequently visited
Breathing as catching up air, hyperventilation

Voice all kinds of pitch heard, Boom! Give me
Xanax please? Yes, that is anxiety, a struggle for self-identity
I ask our LORD to be with me on this episode of uncertainty
That He may give me inner healing and be anxiety-free.

Sometimes I called this anxiety a traitor, because it comes unannounced. Unlike other illnesses they show some signs and symptoms as fever, vomiting and headaches, etc.

But anxiety, attacks in the midst of any season and any occasion unannounced. It is an abrupt emotion and unpleasant feeling as in irritating and bothersome. My anxiety lasted for at least fifteen minutes. I was still thankful it was not a continuous one. In this chaotic world, we need to search for even for a little moment of consolation. For me my consolation was to have a break from feeling anxious, I would settle for that. That's how depressed I was and desperate to feel better.

The following ACRONYM of ANXIETY is just giving us an idea of the scope of everything about anxiety.

A-ngry feelings can't be controlled
N-egative response manifested when anxious
X-anax is the medicine of choice, to calm down an anxious person
I-dentity must be given back to self
E-ngulf the dark world, with
T-rials and challenges
Y-earning to get well to the fullest

The question I asked was, how did I reach the fullness of my wellness? That fits the title of my book, "CLIMB UP WAY UP HIGH"

And I have another ACRONYM that refers to Anxiety

A-n unidentified object feeling inside the brain.
N-o amount of persuasion to calm down
X-out (cross out) all the favorite things, because of no interest at all
I-solating and secluding oneself
E-ngage in unpleasant thoughts
T-rying to cope in every struggle
Y-earning to be back to normal life.

Anxiety attacked me by surprise. Wherever I was and whatever I was doing, it attacked me without any warning. Even when I was in a group like when I attended our Nursing grand reunion, it attacked me and I didn't know what to do. I just ended up going to the washroom and stayed there for a while inside one of the rooms. I was so quiet and I was holding my rosary. I couldn't remember if I was praying. All I knew I had my rosary in my hand. I was thinking that time that if I was at home, I would have already put a lot of vicks vaporub on my forehead. For me it's my magic medicine. I thank GOD all the time that I was able to survive the mini attacks I had. A lot of things going on in my mind that time. Questions like will I ever get well from this? Do other people experience what I am experiencing? Do I look normal to my friends? The final quest was, do I have to live with it?

If the word ANXIETY is a person's name I would choose it as my second middle name. How could I not say this, it does not want to leave me alone.

Well, I guessed I was just climbing up not knowing how high.

DEPRESSION

The sound of silence is now finally heard, after more than two decades ago. And I can come out now from a forceful hibernation.

People suffering from depression are very good in hiding their emotions, getting better in self-denying and best acting in dealing with personal confrontation. Also wearing different kinds of mask.

Many victims of depression are still victims. The reason why there is increase number of mental illness such as depersonalization, anxiety and depression is, because of the ***stigma attached*** is still there.

When I was working as a mental health counselor, I loved doing the group therapy with my clients. I was enjoying my job, not aware that I would be a future candidate and title holder of depression. In our group therapy I was emphasizing that depression was ***treatable***. I even had this acronym as our guide in overcoming depression. I was so energetic giving a lot of examples to motivate them. I was not aware that depression was getting friendlier to me. It became too friendly that few years after, it won my friendship. I was under the spell of depression. My depression was preceded by depersonalization and anxiety first.

I didn't expect that I would have depression because I was a positive person. All I remember, I already quit working as a mental health counselor when I realized I was having depression. I can't remember what triggered my depression?

I just found myself with no appetite when my mother offered me my favorite food. I was already smoking that time and it got worse. I continuously smoked, from one cigarette to another stick. I didn't even use a lighter for the next sticks. Our house was like a chimney.

Symptoms of depression were progressively seen in me. I started to manifest the symptoms of this dreadful illness. I was just like a robot with no insight and my crying spells were terrible. That time I didn't care to take a bath. Embarrassing now that I am thinking of it. I didn't care if I stink, of course not at present time. I smell good now. I was not totally unhygienic because I was surrounded by my love ones who were taking care of me including my hygiene.

Depression for me, I will repeat is a Blessing. A lot of good things happened after that depression ordeal. A productive life and life fulfillment were my rewards (from the struggling and the chaotic self with occasional panic attacks to the surviving stage.) This entails the signs of recovery.

Before I dwell on this unwanted mental illness, let me emphasize that there were two more enemies that came into my life…the depersonalization and the anxiety.

I suffered depersonalization and the anxiety for a long period of time, before this depression hits me. Depression indeed is not picky. The victims of depression were not only ordinary people. I have heard from different people, from the news, and have read the newspapers about depression all over the world. Some were celebrities, some were even relatives of prominent people, even from religious sects, some are teen-agers and some are even senior citizens. Not only that depression is associated with suicides but also with victims of chemical and substance abusers. And these are contributing factors too and considered causes of depression.

Sometimes the word depression is being misused. When someone failed in the driving test you will hear, "I am depressed I didn't make it". Or "I'm depressed I did not get the job." But whatever the reasons of misusing the word depression, still those reasons might be the predisposing factors of the occurrence of depression in the future. So before we suspect someone has a depression we should indeed know what engulfs or surrounds the actual feeling of depression. A depressed person can verbalize lists of how they feel. Allow me to verbalize my own view and concept of depression aside from my actual experiences that I have shared in this book.

Depression is a word of many faces, this is my very own concept.

Depression will stop you from being you.

Depression can tear and wear you down.

Depression is a sad story, yet trying to have a happy one, like a clown, (crying in the inside and laughing on the outside

Depression is the feature of this "tragedy-comedy faces" (the symbol or logo of entertainment)

Depression has no insight, full of fright and plight.

Depression paralyzes an active mind.

Depression was ME. My name is Esther B. Jimenez, I AM a Depression Survivor.

Esther Jimenez

PLIGHT TO FIGHT

Let the climbing begins. I really think seriously and indeed pray about this confession of mine about my traumatic, unforgettable and the "*stigma attached*" experiences. I have the courage now to tell my story especially about my plight in detail to the whole world.

As I have mentioned earlier, the very first episode of my depersonalization plight was when I was in grade school. It was very vivid in my memory of what happened and what I really felt.

This was just a repetition from the first chapter (Who AM I?) I can't help not to tell the same story because this was part of my juvenile struggle.

One night I just woke up and I felt this strange feeling unaware of my surroundings. I approached my father and told him that I was scared to die. I told him this, right after I asked him, "who I was?" Then I asked him if I was going to die. If somebody will ask me now why and where I got these questions, I don't have any idea of what to say. The more I wouldn't know at that very young age. What can a seven year old feel and think with such impertinent questions like the ones I asked. It seemed they were questions of a smart kid? Right? Not really! Those were questions that led me to do this writing now. The bottom line is, this is the reality of anxiety from the point of view of an innocent girl.

To be honest, at this stage of my life (almost third quarter) of the century, I could still recall, remember and rewind that short moment in my life. Years have gone smoothly after that dim moment. My youthful years were not bad at all. Since I was the oldest among the siblings, I pretended at that young age, that I was the leader when we were playing and feeling responsible. We were four then, two girls (me and my sister), and two boys. So we could pass by playing basketball. But we were using a small inflatable plastic ball. It was light and easy to dribble and shoot. In fairness, I was good in boy's game. I was the expert in almost all the boy's games like marble games, rubber bands, toy guns, postcards with images of comic characters and they sometimes called them, "teks". I said expert because I was always winning.

When we played "war", I even had a wooden toy gun, and a wooden sword hooked on my belt (both sides of my waist.) Imagine a little warrior girl. I was a typical "tomboy". I was relaying these children's games and my role, in that childhood life because of the term, "psychodyanamics". I will tackle this topic later on the next pages.

Whatever personality a person has, indeed has something to do with how a person is brought up. That's what we called, psychodynamics. It has something to do with personality development.

My anxiety attack was rooted from my growing up or childhood development. Along the way of my childhood journey, I developed an "identity crisis". I didn't know about these things before. Since I took up Nursing, I learned the terms psychoanalysis, psychodynamics, psychosocial, psychiatric and other medical terms. And of course I've learned the correlation of each.

My high school life was just fair. I finished the four years without sweat. I graduated on time. I didn't have back subjects. I was in the second to the highest section when I graduated. From time to time I was joining my classmate in attending a jam session party (dancing and with snacks of sandwich and soft drinks or juices.) Of course high school "crushes" were in fads. Though I had few crushes among the batchmates, I didn't pay much attention because I was more attentive to my crush in the elementary school, whom I still encountered around that time. He was a nice boy, a young artist and gave me a lot of his own pencil drawings. I enjoyed looking at the cartoon characters that he drew. To be honest there is a smile at my face as I am writing this. Memory is a memory. *First crush never dies".*

High school life for me was a little bit confusing yet it was fun. I also remember during high school that there were at least three or four classmates of mine or batchmates (girls) who had crush on me. I told them I didn't feel the way they feel. Innocently speaking, what did I know about feeling something with the same sex? Now I realize that maybe it was just an admiration. As far as I could remember I was thoughtful and kind when I was in high school. So the "crush" that they mean was admiring my little thoughtful ways.

Well, it was just my high school life. There was not much plight to fight. And yet this tiny incident contributed to my episode of identity crisis. I didn't have episode of anxiety attack the whole four years. So there was no battle of confusion, nor bouts of depersonalization and nor plight to fight.

Next episode was two years after my high school graduation. During those two years, I took up my Pre-Nursing course and at the same time working in a tobacco factory as an ordinary laborer. So between the ages of sixteen to eighteen I was a working student. During that time I was working at the factory and there was this woman, (seven years older than me) that I met. I was seventeen years old then and she was twenty-four years old. She was tomboyish, a very nice friend and thoughtful too. She showed interest in me and she was fond of me, and pursued to court me. I enjoyed her company. We've been closed for two years.

At younger age I was already working hard. I used to wake up at 5:00am, already at the factory at 6:45am. I used to leave work at 3:30pm and already in school at 5:00pm on my first subject. Then, already at home between 9:30pm to 10:00pm. I did this routine for two years. When I finished the two years of Pre-Nursing course, I went for my internship. During this internship my next "depersonalization attack" surfaced. My depersonalization and my anxiety became worse. I started to display duality of behavior. (Warning) I am not schizophrenic. When I said duality of behavior, I meant laughing in the outside, crying in the inside. I put a very nice front (but with the butterflies on my stomach all the time), I could strongly felt the seeming built-in earthquake inside my body. I had this plight for almost two years, without any medication nor treatment.

Sometimes I think I was a "masochist". Everything that happened and every plight I fought, it boiled down to "***stigma attached***". I learned to be accustomed to this plight as my sensitive companion. I was struggling, yet I didn't know what to do. My coping mechanism that time was to let the struggle happened for seconds until it subsided. The stigma attached was, I was worried that people might think something was really wrong with me, especially if they witness my plight.

So mother nature gave me a rest, indeed a long rest. It was a break from the tension, struggle and attacks. This time there was a change of environment. This was a huge change I should say. This was the real plight. I *flew* to the United States of America. This was a flight, a real challenge of plight out to a far distance.

WELCOME TO AMERICA

Enough for my late childhood life and let me proceed further. Let us go out of the country, from my native land to the foreign land. This entails another adjustment.

There's a huge change from miles and miles away from my native land, Philippines. Questions we might ask: Did my plight end? Did the struggle continue? Did you do more fighting? Well, plights, struggles, and fights are just like problems. As long as we live, as long as we are breathing and as long as we exist, those will continue to exist in our life.

From the time I landed on this land of opportunity, something indeed changed. Change of weather, change of daily encounter, change of language, change of life style, and a total change of atmosphere. Did I ever have a cultural shock? No, I didn't have any. Personally, I noticed that it did help me personally this change of environment. Of course, the surroundings were wide and with wide diversion too. For me there would be a lot of destructions? I would like to call it "hidden relief".

Yes, I was relieved, yet sometimes Mr. Anxiety was visiting me, alternating with (Miss D.), Depersonalization. I was surprised I haven't met (Mrs. D.), Depression that time yet. The changes that happened were the destructions that aided me in my defense to my plight.

If you are in Rome, "do what the Romans do." This is a saying that will not be missed to do by a working visa holder. So, most of us who arrived that time here in the United States learn how to drive. Learning to drive was a plus in my life achievement. I could go wherever my friends and me would like to go, as far as interstate driving was concerned. Not only that I learned how to drive, I learned a bad habit too. I learned to smoke while driving and had been a chain smoker. I enjoyed that habit (that time.)

Before I went to the United States I said "yes" to a suitor that became my boyfriend and committed to be my sweetheart who was my batchmate in high school. So while I was in Little Rock, Arkansas, the first State I landed on, I had a boy friend. I was in that state for less than three years.

One ironic incident happened in my life there was I didn't pass the Stateboard Examination. I passed the four subjects, but not the Psychiatric Nursing subject.

This is the irony. I just missed two points from the passing grade. That time I was planning to go home. My boy friend was adamantly asking me to go home. We had plans to get married and he would do all this proposal thing back home.

This was another trial on my part, to make a major decision. I had to choose between retaking the State Board Examination or going back home for the wedding plans. Definitely I was excited to go home and to get married. So my friends and co-workers gave me a "bridal shower" and a "*despedida*" party (a going home party), before I left for the Philippines.

I arrived in Manila, Philippines on June 10, 1976 and saw my loved ones again, my parents, brothers, sister, my grandmother and the rests of my relatives. But most of all I saw my near future groom and met his immediate relatives as well.

On our first day of reunion, we discussed the wedding plans, we didn't agree of the date. When I was still in the states, we agreed to have our wedding on June of that year. He would like to move it on December of the same year. It was ok, I didn't have problem with that. Actually the problem was not the date. It was more personal than that. Since I have already started to confess almost every personal aspect of my life, maybe this won't hurt me and my ego. Well, this is regarding being conservative and standing for ones principle. I am not going into the details here. Let me just share these two major principles of mine regarding relationship. I want to get married "pure and untouched" and "not to have a child out of wedlock.

And here is the scenario. *If we were moving the date and planning to get married at later date, I must stick with my principle of to marry as a pure bride (untouched). We didn't see eye to eye in that particular situation. My being upright to my principles have caused the break-up. What if I get pregnant not married, so a child out of wedlock will be the result. My principle is stronger than the unwanted consequences.*

By the way this happened in a span of two weeks, since I arrived home. Don't judge me if the wedding plans didn't go through. I didn't have any regrets at all. I knew that time that it was a foolish pride. *But I believed that if you love your principles and moral values you will live your life with integrity.*

Parting ways was never my plan. But we were in our adjustment period. My principles were pushing me to decide on what is the right thing to do? That time the right thing to do was to part ways. There were more to my principles, but pride made me firm. *(Did I really do the right thing?)*

I didn't see my life having an ideal family after that. It gave me a moral lesson instantly. I went on and since I was also in an adjustment period, I took the chance of my adrenalin push by planning things constructively.

I would admit, there was a wound inside my heart, but I have a GOD that would help me get healed. I didn't have time to dwell on wasting my time. *"Life Goes On"*

Esther Jimenez

KILL THE TIME

I guessed the factors that contributed to my depersonalization and anxiety were the incidents happened when I was in the States. I will explain the relevance of me, not passing the board exam with my identity crisis. I found this relevance after twenty years ago, but this will be (back to the future). This will be told or mention as we go along with my chronological part of my story. Meantime let me just continue my journey to the center of my story.

After breaking up with my ex-boyfriend I pursued my studies, (just to kill the time). I am an expert in murdering my time. I was always thinking of "what's next?" I did not waste my time so I enrolled full load subjects and took up Bachelor of Science in Nursing Supplemental. It took me two years to graduate. This is how I killed my time. I did a lot of thesis. I took this course while I was waiting for my visa for my immigrant petition. It looked like my waiting would take longer than I expected so, I tried to look for more things to achieve.

There was a group of Saudian from the Ministry of Health arrived in Manila to recruit medical staff, of course including nurses. I applied for a year contract. It did not take long we flew to the Kingdom of Saudi Arabia. So another place, another challenge and I was expecting another plight. When I went to America, the communication was better because it is an English speaking country and I can speak English. Saudi Arabia is Saudi Arabia and very few people can understand and speak English. Either you are good and know how to do sign language, that is one way to be able to communicate. Or maybe there would be an interpreter or have a friend or a Filipino co-worker who had been there longer. What I did was I started asking whomever I encountered and I forced myself to learn and to speak their language. I had a notebook that I used and I started jotting down words with the translations. I memorized ten words a day and I spoke the words I learned and practiced them everyday.

Before I go on with my experience/story there was a slight plight happened. When we reached the land of the Kingdom, we were placed temporarily by the Ministry of Health in the hospital in Riyadh (one of the main cities). We waited for our assignment places. We were less than fifty Filipinos recruited; from the midwives, x-ray technicians, nurses and physicians. To my surprise, my name was called and unfortunately my assignment was in a remote place called "Turaif". I was separated from the large group. I started crying and asking them (the people in charged) that I wanted to go home. Since I have heard strange stories about the culture involving foreigners I kept my mouth shut and I started praying in my heart. So the road trip begun. I have experienced seeing the desert around and some citizens riding on camels. The Saudian driver with turban on his head was so nice but we couldn't understand what he was saying. There were three Filipinos in the car like an army jeepney with me. The other nurse was going to a place called, "Al Qobar" also a remote place. The two Filipino guys were x-ray technicians and they would go to a place near Jordan. The only consolation I had was I was the first drop. It was almost sunset when I arrived to my destined place. It was a pretty good size clinic, with the nurses' quarter at the upper level. A woman wearing black with her face covered with black veil-like, greeted me, "Marhaba", now I know the meaning of that. It means "welcome or hi! ". There were two Filipino staff residing in the boarding house, one was a nurse and the other was a midwife. Everyday of my stay there was significant in a way that I felt I was in another planet.

I won't go through the details of my experiences there. Some were interesting, but most were unpleasant. One of the reasons was loneliness and homesickness. All I can say was I was assigned to be an assistant to a Syrian dentist who understood a little bit of English. With his limited English and my striving Arabic self-study, both of us filled the space of nothingness. He was teaching me the different parts of the body in Arabic, also the numbers, the colors, and the common greetings. I was surprised that in three months I was able to talk to the patients. The dentist called me,"*shatra, and with fi mokh*" which means I was smart and with brain. What a compliment. The truth was I really wanted to learn their language so I can give better care to the patient. My principle was, "how can you give a better care if it was only sign languages". The irony was, it was not even sign language for the deaf and mute. It was a bedside nursing care that needed quality care. Patients deserved to be understood and vice versa. I believed that with better communication there will be better nursing care.

Again, my mind was busy working on a request of transfer. I was requesting to be transferred from the clinic to the hospital. Through the small knowledge of how to communicate with them I was able to work on this request. But the only way I would be allowed to transfer was if I had an exchange staff from the main hospital in "Al Quarayat". The name of the hospital is King Faisal Hospital. I was just fortunate to know that one of the nurses would like to be in Turaif because her husband was working there. After three months the transfer was approved with the help of my superior, the dentist. It was not all unpleasant. Learning another language for me is a blessing and a fulfillment. Even up to present time I could get by, speaking Arabic.

I could communicate with an Arabic speaking person. I was enjoying communicating with the patient. As I have mentioned previously, I can't tell in details about my experiences there. I respect their religion and other cultures. I managed to stay in a place where I didn't go out for socialization for at least eighteen months. Women were not allowed to go without covering their faces. Even foreigners were not allowed to just go out. They also have to cover their faces It is "*mamnuh*" it means forbidden to show a woman's face. It is "*haram*" and it means prohibited to go around with uncovered face.

My transfer was a success but there were more encounters because there were more workers, more intrigues, more plights and more challenges. Since I can speak better than some of them, I was subjected to an intrigue of envy and jealousy, which I have learned to manage and handled fairly square. After eighteen months my US visa immigrant petition arrived and I have to migrate to America. You see I killed my time pleasantly and accomplished something fruitfully and productively. The benefits of enthusiasm and curiosity are knowledge, wisdom and blessings. This is a gentle way of killing the time. I will change "killing the time" to love myself and make use of myself and my time productively. Time is so precious and we should value the time allotted to us to be productive.

BACK TO USA

I left the Kingdom of Saudi Arabia with honor and pride knowing how to speak their language. As I have mentioned my visa immigrant petition arrived so I needed to migrate to the United States of America. This time I landed in the windy city, a busy city of Chicago, Illinois.

I didn't work as a nurse because I didn't have an RN licensure. So I couldn't land a nurse job. Do you want to know something about Esther? It is only through this book that some of my friends, some classmates, and some relatives will find out the greatest "resume" ever submitted. Yes, it is Esther's job history. You will be able to find out why I did have such a long list of resume. I was the master of resume submission.

I started to apply for an office job position in the Nursing Home. I was hired and stayed there for few months. Another office job was a Medical Record Director. I was hired again but stayed there for few months, too. I did apply for sales positions in advertising media.

Instead of mentioning a vast number of institutions, companies and hospitals, let me just be direct to the point. The truth is, this is really a public confession. Only few people know that I had, shall I say a terrible resume, a horrific one and unbelievable job history. I would say maybe less than seven people were aware of my more than fifty lists of job interviews.

At the moment I am feeling embarrassed and ridiculed with my own confession. But what can I do, this is the truth of my life's fate (the subtle journey of my life) I am sad while I am writing the facts about my life; how can it happen to a professional nurse like me? I am not only a professional one but indeed a good nurse. It was indeed frustrating to be in that situation.

Since I could not find a nurse job, I tried to apply as a mental health counselor. I was hired because of my nursing background. As far as I could remember this job lasted longer than my previous jobs. I enjoyed my job as a mental health counselor. My job descriptions were to handle a group therapy, to do a 1:1 session with a client, to admit and to discharge the clients. The nice thing in working as a mental health counselor is the fulfillment I was feeling when I hear the clients and even some of my co-workers complimenting my work as to the way I handled my job. This is one vivid memory in my life. Indeed it helped me in my coping-healing struggle.

Everytime I did a group therapy I was satisfied, because I had a good group participation and there were positive feedback from the patients. I remember in one of the group therapies, we discussed about depression. I was so excited because I felt fulfilled seeing them the way they responded, (with insights and full of hopes.) I loved to write acronyms and I created an acronym from the word "Depression". This acronym became the "brown bag" of the clients. Here is the brown bag for all of us;

> D-well on good and pleasant memories
> E-ducation: like the medical regimen and psychotherapy
> P-ositive thinking is important
> R-ise up from feeling down and keep on living
> E-nding life is never a solution
> S-adness you will feel, but you can overcome and you will
> S-eek for help, share your feelings and reach out.
> I-gnore your negative thoughts
> O-utlook in life should always be positive
> N-ever say there is no treatment for depression, for there is. It is ***treatable.***

There it is my encounter of depression. And I addressed this to a group therapy.

Working in the mental institution or mental health department of a hospital was the longest period I had in my list of job history. I worked in three different hospitals in the span of two and a half years, staying maybe for three to seven months. My job history was erratic yet it seemed I enjoyed or rather I was comfortable working as a mental health counselor.

By the way while I was working as a mental health counselor, I was also working part time as a sales representative selling advertising space ads in one of the local newspapers. I did this for a year in this windy city. I have been in this city of Chicago since 1981. From that time and up to few years ago, I have been feeling edgy, anxious and irritable.

While I was working as a mental health counselor, I was not aware that I might be suffering from a depression.

I think I owe you an explanation why did I have such immense number of resumes One reason was I couldn't handle working with the co-workers who were rude, lazy, and with unpleasant attitudes (those who were mean to patients.) Another reason was, I couldn't handle stressors in my life. There were times, I felt strange in my own silent self. I always felt depersonalized. The whole scenario of my erratic job history was an indication of my impending illness, (the popular mental health problem), called "Depression." Actually the problems lie on the relationship with everybody, with the co-workers. The way I deal with my co-workers, the way I see things, and the principles that I have, I was very sensitive and I was very observant. I easily get frustrated with a lot of things because of my expectations were a little higher than the rests of the people.

I was indeed aware of all these things. And I know I was not like that before. I was a good nurse and a real good worker. I even received a recognition award for my performance. I was also given a certificate of perfect attendance before I graduated in Nursing. *Then, what happened?* It was confirmed that I was suffering from Depression. This was the start of my Depression ordeal, when I got back to USA.

Esther Jimenez

DISCOVERY

After working as a mental health counselor for more than a year, from the last hospital employer, I decided to finally quit. Then I continued to work as a salesperson, selling advertising space ads. I was happy with my decision to quit from the salaried full time job. I thought selling advertising space ads was better because it was a commission basis. I didn't need to force my self according to the schedule. I can work in my own time. Since then I felt better working with no pressure and no forceful commitment. So there was already clarity of why my job history was unstable. Why such jobs turn over were fast and fluctuating? And why I had erratic job history? The bottom line was my depersonalization and anxiety never left me. They were with me since I was seven years old.

As I have mentioned previously, I still was experiencing the anxiety and depersonalization. It felt like I had a twin shadowing me wherever I went. This is why I was still facing the uncertainties, facing my dim moments and facing my hidden attacker.

I mentioned earlier that I learned to smoke again. I remember while I was dealing with my twins (depersonalization and anxiety), I was also in the midst of discovering something already infront of me. That is the mystery of depression. Many years have passed-by, the depression was also passing me by. Then it visited me the year 1995. When the depression visited me, I felt depersonalized. I could hardly calm myself and my anxiety was competing with its sudden attack. Then I lost my appetite to eat. I started to feel exhausted. I get easily irritated. The worst thing was I smoked continuously. People at home noticed there were ash trays in all rooms and some corners of the rooms; in the washroom, in the basement and in the porch. All the ash trays were filled with cigarette butts. I was pretty sure I stunk like a skunk and I was like a walking chimney because of the cigarettes' smokes. I started to isolate myself. I was having sleepless nights. Actually, I wasn't sleeping at all, nor eating.

That was a call for me to call for help.

My mother was crying as I was crying too. She was touching my head and stroking my hair and praying over me. She even gave me a warm sponge bath and put talcum powder on my back, to my upper and lower extremities. She knew that I love Vicks Vaporub on my head and she massaged my forehead with vicks.

We decided to have a family meeting for we felt I needed to see a professional. So, we had a family meeting (with my mother, my cousin, and my brother from another States via the telephone line.) The rests of the family were in our country. But we were updating them of the plans through overseas call. So, we decided that I would be seeing a professional, (a psychologist or a psychiatrist.) We made appointments with a recommended psychologist and a psychiatrist. I was the one who chose my psychiatrist. I knew him when I was still working as a mental health counselor.

I saw my psychologist first. During the initial visit, all I did was to cry. I didn't talk much. I was shaking and felt so exhausted. At first I had to see him twice a week. Then once a week, I still have to see my psychiatrist.

My psychiatrist was the one who gave me prescriptions of Xanax (anti-anxiety) and Prozac (anti-depressant). I had been seeing him at least once a week too.

The next time I visited my psychologist I was already a little bit calmer. I was able to pour out my "strange and weird" feelings. I used the words "strange and weird" because that's how I felt. I felt I was out of the world. Just felt uneasy, uncomfortable and unreal. I felt I was a stranger with everything in a strange world.

So much for these two professional guys who would study my brain and behavior. This was my thinking after meeting them. Sometimes I was hesitant to see them. Maybe that feeling was a part of my illness, trying to avoid people. Unfair to both of them, I should not give them up and I should give myself and them a chance, right? So the therapy continued. I was seeing them every month, thirty minutes with my psychologist and forty-five minutes with my psychiatrist. Aside from the prescribed medications I was taking, the 1:1 session was also a big help. During the therapy session, there were many thoughts going on in my mind. Of course I was telling them all my unpleasant thoughts, too.

Finally, I found out that I have been treated for my *Depersonalization, Anxiety, and Depression.* That is why I created the acronym (D.A.D.) So with the new discovery of me having depression I can now admit that my name is *Esther B. Jimenez, I have a Depression.* Now that the depression in me has surfaced I have to deal with it daily. This was the thought I had when I found out that not only that I have anxiety and depersonalization, but this awful illness joined the two buddies. It was very, very clear that I was suffering from depression. What a "discovery"?

STEPS TO RECOVERY

Steps are guides that would help a person to the road to recovery, may it be The Twelve Steps or any guiding steps and even the basic one, two, three steps. It is indeed a guide that would help a person to the right pathway, the road to recovery.

Situations like these that needed treatment or needed solutions to existing problems, I think "copycat" is beneficial. If it is something that can help healed someone, doing things that have already been tried and it worked, why not do the same thing? I am referring to my own road to recovery, to my own destiny and to my own ways of survival. What am I talking about here? Yes, I am talking about the famous Twelve Steps Program of the group called, (AA group), Alcoholic Anonymous. It is not exactly copycat, because I didn't follow every steps they have. It was only about the submission of self to the power greater than ourselves.

Before I found out that I was suffering from depression, I already was praying for my healing. Part of my spiritual aspect that time was, I joined a Catholic Charismatic Life Seminar. It was a thirteen-week session.

I had an awkward experience on my first two weeks. While I was listening to the Christian speaker, I was attentive (I thought), but nothing was going into my head. It was indeed paradoxical, listening and yet writing notes (actually I was just doodling.) Come to think of it now, it is so embarrassing.

Well, that's not what I was supposed to tell as my awkward experience. The thing that I was going to say was, *right after the last Christian song, before we adjourned, (this was one of the nights during the life seminar)I was rushing to get into my car and lit a cigarette, then another one, then another one, until I got home.* So, I guessed smoking was part of my therapy (I thought). Again, if I am thinking about it right now, I will cover my face from embarrassment.

I have a Catholic confession to tell. I had my rosary in my pocket, but I never said my rosary that time. This was not intentional. I was not aware of what was going on in my life. My thinking that time was, it would protect me by just holding it or by having it in my pocket as within my reach. It was a total embarrassment on my part. To confess my brief present spiritual status, *(praying rosary is my life now.)*

Nobody knew how I was feeling then and what was I was suffering from? I didn't tell anyone. BUT ONLY GOD THE ALMIGHTY KNEW everything, my Higher power).

I wasn't ready to tell anyone, yet. But I had one or two close friends and my cousin that I trusted. I was honest enough to reveal part of my being to them.

I started to journal my everyday encounters, my thoughts and my activities. The contents of my journal were all unpleasant, negative and full of indescribable pain in my head, (not headache, not migraine but air tight and feeling empty-headed).

In my journal book, I was writing the date, the time, about my no appetite, my smoking, my not sleeping, not to forget my depersonalization attack and my anxiety attack and of course my depression is within me all day long and all night long. The D.A.D. (Depersonalization, Anxiety and Depression) was my friendly enemy.

There were moments that I was in my normal self. If I attain these moments, I was taking advantage indeed of the moments and I listened to the music.

On the eleventh week of the Christian Life Program, I quit smoking, a cold turkey cessation. So, good-bye Mr. Slim Benson Hedges (my brand)

The Christian Life Program was in the evening so I could still see my psychologist and my psychiatrist. Part of the Christian Life Program was the sharing time. When it was my turn to share I just shared my anxiety and depression. I left out the depersonalization. They won't understand the feeling of being depersonalized.

One thing I was very appreciative in my history of mental illness was, I wasn't confined in any mental institution. This was another **stigma attached**. Being hospitalized as a mentally-ill patient was a big impact to the mentally-ill clients versus the community. In the first place it won't happen because I won't allow it. That is the advantage of being a nurse. A nurse knows the consequences. I didn't like the idea of being one of the clients falling in line for the medications and after that, checking the mouth if the medicines were swallowed or not. I was thinking of the movie, "One Flew Over The Cuckoo's Nest". One by one they were given their medications. It wasn't therapeutic for me. I guessed the **"stigma attached"** was in my thoughts. Anyway, I was glad I reached out and I was not confined. I knew I had a long way to go yet. So just relax and wait for more plight and insight of Esther's D.A.D. (Depersonalization, Anxiety and Depression) challenge.

This thirteen week Christian Life Program had helped me a lot. Part of the program too, was a group discussion about anything that you wanted to share. This was healthy because we were surrounded by prayerful brothers and sisters in CHRIST.

I remember Dr. Robert Schuller's quotation, "inch by inch is a cinch". It gets easier if you take things as step by step.

The journaling, the Christian Life Program, the sharing from the heart, the listening to good music, the interacting with friends and with the good influential people, and the prayers most of all, were the actual steps to the road to recovery.

Few good things happened after two and a half months and this needed to be shared. I quit smoking, hygiene awareness came back, appetite also was back and insomnia stayed in one corner. While we are now in the insomniac topic, I would like to share the poem I wrote when Mr. Insomnia was bugging me at night.

INSOMNIAC SYNDROME

Sleepless nights, staring at the ceiling restless
non-stop yawning, teary-eyed Yes, that's me

having insomniac syndrome, Feeling light-headed,
eyes deep-droopy; I need help to sleep, I pray hard
to have my sleep back, I uttered, "Hail Mary",
Many times, I called St. Anthony to find my sleep
(the Saint for finding losing something), And I asked the Holy Spirit to interfere, LORD GOD, prayers are indeed powerful. Now I am back to my sleep norm, I can dream again and back to my regular snore; Good-bye to my insomniac syndrome. *What a relief to verbalize my thoughts and feelings. This helped me a lot. So let us Climb Up more, Way up High.*

Esther Jimenez

SHARE-SHARE A RIDE

Am I willing to share fully about this depression of mine? I was talking to myself and I was asking myself, was I selfish? Do I need to share my dim moments? My identity crisis? My uncertainties? Do the people need to know about my depression?

I would always like to see for myself (the intention of a certain decision) before I blurt out. This time, I know I need to share. I must share and I love to share. It's just like share-share a ride. If I share fully, I will also find out if "Mr. Stigma" will hinder or will intercept my sharing.

I feel comfortable now to share with friends, acquaintances and mind you even with the strangers. Yes, it's true I can sense a stranger who is reaching out and I won't be hesitant to extend my empathy, my help and my full understanding. And it did happen to me in three occasions.

One was, when I was in the church and after the mass I heard a lady at the back of the pew crying. I prayed before I approached her. I realized she was very lonely and seemed to be a little bit restless. The words I heard were, "I don't want to live anymore". She was expressing of wanting to end her life. So I sat beside her and I was just listening. I was just waiting for the right time for me to say something. I mentioned about my struggle, my coping and my surviving. We exchanged numbers and the next time we met, she was feeling better. This is the power of sharing, the self-less effect.

Another incident was a young lady approached me after I gave a short talk about depression. She admitted that she was a victim of depression. And she can relay to what I have shared to the group.

She asked me if I could talk to her husband, because he had been so quiet and seemed to be crying most of the time. She found out about my sharing one time before the Holy Week. An instance like this I can't just ignore. I called this, "opportunity", the chance to share and a chance to be heard and mostly a chance for inner healing. Sharing for me is a climbing up-way up high.

When I shared my life during my talk on my 70th birthday, November of last year, two people approached me after my talk. One was the wife of a family member and the other was one of the guests.

The wife of a family member asked me what did I do when I started to feel depressed. Since I didn't share the detail of what happened to me, I just told her that she can call me anytime. I didn't ignore her question, but I insinuated that we can talk more. She was appreciative and the way I looked at her, she seemed to see an open door that she can come in and feeling safe. It was a great feeling for me too, seeing people like her. It was just sharing a boat on a sailing trip. As of the present time, we are communicating with each other and getting in touch through the facebook, sending also photos of her daughter. She seemed having fun with her family. I reassured her to call me anytime just to share. Sharing indeed works.

One of the guests of my sister was diagnosed with Major Depression, according to her, when she approached me and talked to me. Only one question that she asked. She just asked me if she could stop taking her anti-depressant medicine. I told her that she should not stop taking any of her medication without consulting her doctor. I learned from my psychiatrist not to stop taking medicines without the doctor's knowledge, plus being a nurse it was a force of habit not to give medical advice regarding medications except for giving instructions when patients were discharged from the hospital.

What these two did was commendable because this was a step to reaching out (actually) an important step in the process of healing for depression.

Sharing is not only from a person or to a person you know. It could be from somebody who is a celebrity, or maybe someone who writes an article about their experience of suffering from depression and maybe a speaker from an organization sponsoring mental health awareness. Sharing is caring. You share your experience for self-awareness and for more insights or virtues to be cultivated.

Few years ago, at least two decades ago I was hesitant to even join a conversation with the topic about depression or any mental illness.

Now, I am willing to share 100% and even the most personal aspect of my life regarding depression, I can speak about it. I want to let the world know that "depression" is ***treatable***. I want to share every page of my story, if it would benefit the recipients of healing, betterment and self-improvement. It's also a great feeling to share a ride. Sharing is a Blessing. So when I share my story, my experience, and my mental health/ illness life, I entrusted our Almighty GOD to allow me to do this sharing for the sake of mankind's sanity. Let us share- share a ride. It is helping me to climb up way up higher.

There is one rule that we follow, when the sharing part started. And the rule is applicable in all group therapy, even in 1:1 session. Whatever is discussed or shared in the group should be confidential. The sharer must know that everything that is being shared is just for the ears of who are in the group and it is just within the four corners of the room. Confidentiality builds confidence and trust in the group and in themselves too.

Actually, sharing is a ventilation. It is venting out the heavy burden. Sharing is therapeutic. Definitely, there is sharing in climbing as to giving points or tips in doing so. More sharing heard and spoken made the climbing easier, to go up higher.

MENTAL HEALTH COUNSELING

Mental health counseling is one of the treatments for a depressed client. So after reaching out and agreeing that I needed a professional help I submitted myself to a mental health counseling. I consulted a psychologist and a psychiatrist. This psychologist was recommended by a social worker whom I worked with. And the psychiatrist was one of the doctors in the hospital where I worked. I met him through his visits to his clients. I trusted the two professionals and I was comfortable with them. Seeing a psychologist and a psychiatrist is very much different from seeing a medical physician. When I see a medical doctor, all I can say is to describe my pains and discomforts just like that. BUT when you talk to a psychologist or a psychiatrist I have to dig deeper not only on my physical discomforts but more on what was I thinking. I have to answer on the how, what, why, where and when questions. To be honest, I felt like it was penetrating my brain especially on the first few visits. I did understand that they have to know more and deeper so I can be counselled properly. Another key word here is *psychodynamics*. It deals more on the emotions, behaviors, human feelings and relational aspects of an individual. So I have to be honest with what I really felt and everything about what was in my mind. I know that in every behavior there is a root or cause of such behavior.

Since one of my problems was sleepless nights and restlessness, I was given by my psychiatrist two prescriptions (Xanax for my insomnia and restlessness and Prozac an antidepressant.)

I was diagnosed with Depression secondary to Chemical Imbalance. I will say it simply how the Prozac works in a body of a patient with depression. This drug is a member of (SSRI) selective serotonin reuptake inhibitors. It balances the serotonin, and serotonin (is one of the neurotransmitters affected in depression.) It helps to make it function properly. So that is the mechanism in which I am not going into detail.

I was learning something during the psychotherapy. I was taking my medications religiously. But to be honest, I didn't take much of Xanax because I didn't want to depend on tranquilizers or any sedatives.

My being a mental health counselor helped me in treating my own mental illness. Before I could hardly say the word "mental illness" addressed to myself. But now I can say "my mental illness". I don't know why, but I feel a relief by just admitting that I am suffering from a mental illness. I can mention the phrases "my mental illness" or "I have a mental illness" as often as I want to, unlike before. Now, I can own it as my personal property, "my mental illness".

One of the things that I benefitted from mental health counseling was the effect or advantage of "verbalization". I realized the value and essence of the continuation of communication or 1:1 session.

Mental health counseling was necessary and very important because it helps in the assessment, diagnosing the client and acquiring the proper treatment. I strongly believed that having a 1:1 session with the professionals were beneficial. Whether a client talked less or a talkative one, it does not matter. As long as you are there in the room feeling safe, not only physically but your secrets are safe too. Nothing is wasted. As I write this and as I ponder on what I am writing I know that nothing was wasted during my time of mental health counseling.

Since I was given an anti-depressant (Prozac) I would say it balanced my serotonin after at least seven months. The psychiatrist discontinued the Prozac after seven months. What an early recovery? Amazing result with very good prognosis!

My psychologist on the other hand was very informative, explaining to me something regarding *identity crisis and depersonalization*. He told me the story of Scarlet A (the movie). It was a story of trying to search for the person's identity. My doctor emphasized that it was only a letter. The reason he said it was only a letter was because I have mentioned to him the impact on me (not being an RN (Registered Nurse.)

In my first few sessions with him, I verbalized my sentiments of not being an RN, here in the states, that brought part of my misery. A misery of hating (not able to work as an RN.) My doctor explained to me that RN is only a group of letters like the one in the movie Scarlet A. He said that the most important thing is to love my being (self.) So part of my depersonalization rooted from just the two letters (RN.) So he gave me an insight about the initials that they are only letters and I should not let the letters ruin my life.

My ill-feelings and sentiments linger longer and had not been resolved until I learned to love myself.

After almost a year, my psychologist gently informed me that he would terminate our session for he felt I was already doing better. It hurts a little bit because of the bonding and fellowship we had. So at least my therapy was a success, as far as this therapy with my psychologist was concerned. I still had to continue my session with my psychiatrist. Mental health counseling is another way to climb up, higher up.

KEEP GOING

After at least seven months of taking my anti-depressant medicine (Prozac), it was discontinued by my psychiatrist. And this time my psychologist also terminated his service for according to his observation and evaluation, I was feeling better.

The show must go on. My treatment went on with my psychiatrist. This was indeed a long treatment. While I was having this psychotherapy, I was not working, I was just at home. I quitted from working as a mental health counselor.

I started journaling and everything I did was in my journal book. Regarding the sales job? Well, was I trying to work on with my enthusiasm? My courage? My Reality check? My fear of the unknown? I still have bouts of uncertainties, depersonalization and once in a while my anxiety attacks. I tried to be patient and be positive and most of all be compliant.

I kept going on because life must go on. Sometimes I wonder what had happened in my life? Why did I become depressed? I never expected that I would be in this situation. I was a go getter woman, aggressive, assertive, strong and a positive person. What causes this depression? Generally speaking, genetic is one of them. Occurrence of stress, grief, sudden loss, divorce, financial problems, prolong illness and, heartbrokenness etc. are also causes of depression. In my case, I didn't have a major reason or cause of my depersonalization, anxiety, and depression. All I know was there was an origin and that's why this book will help me find out everything that entails the depression especially my own depression.

My father had a history of nervous breakdown when he was young at age. So, it's a give-away statement. Genetic is one of the causes of my own mental illness. The next cause is "identity crisis" which I have already mentioned. I was dwelling on the fact that I wasn't able to work as a registered nurse that long. Whatever happened, already happened. I should keep going and going on what it is I am doing. In climbing up and reaching higher we should keep going, otherwise we'll be stuck in the middle of climbing and we won't be able to reach our goal, to reach the peak of success. So I had to keep going.

On my part, I did my best to climb up high. (I strove hard to get healed) I surrendered everything to our Almighty, my ultimate and forever Savior.

I could feel I am having my insight back. Now that I feel spiritually uplifted, I can feel my healing.

Being positive and acknowledging our Almighty's help and guidance I am grateful and appreciative. Despite of the dark moments that engulfed me, I was given the chance to rise up and climb up high.

The key to everything you wanted to accomplish, to any goals you wanted to reach and to any obstacles you wanted to overcome, is not to stop but to Keep Going. We should continue to strive more. In my case, mine is going up high. So let's **Keep Going**. Every time I encounter this "phrase keep going" it reminds of the bunny that keeps drumming while walking.

Had I stop being positive in dealing with my daily encounters, my world will stop too and I will be nowhere to be found. Maybe I will be in the oblivion of worthless creature. I have experienced to lose my will not only the will per se but the will to live. This is indeed the outlook that this depression would like the world to see. But thank you to the world of beauty (beautiful creatures, creations and wonderful life) that we failed to see. Most importantly thank you for the power of "**Keep Going**", the power of not wanting to stop. This is one of the things I realized in this climbing up, that I should keep going.

I AM A CLIMBER

I have mentioned in the Introduction about my conversation with my *physical therapist* who is also a rock climber. I learned from her that there was a fulfillment that she felt every time she reached the top of the wall or rock.

There are more things into climbing up and I just want to tackle more about it. Let me reiterate myself that climbing helped me feel empowered.

Literally, climbing is very difficult. For me I couldn't do it. And I won't do it. But climbing is a very good guide, a very good example, and a very good analogy when you want to overcome a fear, when you want to reach a goal and when you are challenge to survive a heavy burden. Each step in climbing is empowering, each step-up in climbing, is one successful achievement and climbing has helped me focused on getting healed.

In climbing there is no hindrance, except not trying it. Disability is not a hindrance. There are climbers who have one arm, or one leg, but this does not hinder them to climb. My disability is different from a regular disability which there are no disabled limbs. In my case only the thought process is a little bit damaged by the D.A.D. Challenge (Depersonalization, Anxiety and Depression.)

I finally have accepted I have disability. It only shows that I am no longer in denial. I realized this when I surrendered myself to the oblivion of dim moments and when I said, "I am Esther, I am a Depression Survivor." When I admitted earlier that my name is Esther, it's only my name. Now when I said, "I am Esther," I am claiming my healing. I was a struggling climber. I learned every step in going up, through the measures I took to survive like the seeing of a psychiatrist, joining the group therapy, journaling, and support of the family and friends. My climbing was easier through my acceptance of my mental disability.

There are facts to know about climbing. One of the facts in wall climbing is, it is difficult to get into the crag first of all. A crag is a steep or rugged cliff or rock face. It is simply a cliff, a ridge and a peak. In comparison to wall climbing is, if it is difficult to get into a crag, it is difficult to admit that we have depression. But I finally did. I did not know what would really entail this admission of (me), to have a mental illness such as depression, yet I boldly admit that I did have depression. That is the most difficult thing to do, but I got over it. If you have grabbed the crag, the worse thing is over. You can focus now to the second step. Like admitting having a depression, it is a relief, and you can focus on the next move. Another fact is feeling disappointed, that is not able to fulfill the activities or any measures related to recovery. Typical example is, those victims of alcoholism maybe feeling disappointed by not able to go further in the Twelve Steps they were following. The ultimate fact is, rock climbing or wall climbing is not just a sport, or a hobby that involves physique. It is also therapeutic. Climbing up is an analogy to a struggling soul suffering from depression or any mental illness. Climbing up has helped people to keep their mind and heart open. In my own case, I was feeling disappointed. I was feeling the disappointments every time I was being attacked by the D.A.D. (Depersonalization, Anxiety and Depression), but I didn't want to give up. If I were an alcoholic and following the Twelve Steps, I will make sure I will reach almost to the last steps. Then the disappointments will be eliminated. I understand that it easy say and done, until I am indeed an alcoholic.

I know that I am just saying this, to make me feel better. But the truth was, whatever steps to follow to recovery, it is not easy. We indeed need a lot of support, massive and fervent prayers and sincere effort and willingness to get well and better.

As a human being, I acknowledged the struggles, the trials, the difficulties are parts of my existence and that I needed to climb up way up high.

Yes, I am A Climber, not literally, but allegorically. Indeed a Depression Survivor.

Climb Up Way Up High

THE OUTCOME IS REWARDING

Reaching ones goal is fulfilling. Achieving the best award is uplifting. Being at the peak through climbing is rewarding.

It is indeed a great feeling if you succeed in every trials, challenges and struggles that you have gone through.

Sometimes we needed to be appreciated and needed to be heard. Support of the family played a very big role in the successful recovery and inner healing of a depressed client.

I am blessed I have that kind of support. I strongly feel the love and support of my family, my loved ones. My mother always prayed over me. My father was always willing to listen and he even knew (the very first episode of my anxiety attack) that I needed to see a professional. He was the one who accompanied me to see the psychiatrist. All my brothers and my one and only sister were very caring and supportive. And of course their fervent prayers were effective. Their phone calls were helpful. The cards, the letters and the flowers that my nieces and nephews sending me helped to cheer me up. Reading their notes and letters made me look for the brighter sides of life and made me feel insightful. They made me see myself in a positive way and encouraged me to love myself more. I can't help but share the following poem that my nephew wrote for me. He dedicated this poem for me. It was so uplifting and I almost forget that I was a special person that loved by GOD and everyone. I must say that I am flattered by his kind thoughts about me. He wrote this poem with sincerity of heart and profound love. He handed this to me about eight years ago (2010). I became bold to face the overwhelming description of my nephew about his aunt "ESTHER." It did help me to overcome my depersonalization. I thank you Francis from the bottom of my heart. (*This is unedited, original as it is.*)

This alphabet helps me to love myself more and better. All I need to do is to re-read, review and remember the love of Our CREATOR for me.

THE ALPHABET OF ESTHER

A-rtist, adviser…in every stroke of her brush shows the color of her sides, as deep as her advices, as strong as the ocean tides.

B-odyguard…she's everyone's protector, ready to battle war, she's guardian by your side, watching over from afar.

C-hef, collector…finder of new recipes, a cook for satisfaction human vault of beauty of crafts, of grand collection.

D-ecision Maker…a firm disposition she has pursuing a single road with certainty and valor, a true marked of an endowed.

E-valuator…appreciative of good things, a critic with good judgement aura of her womanhood.

F-riendly…her spirit of attraction, magnet of companionship, hooking both comrades and fish, she reels the rod of friendship, a fisherman indeed.

G-ame player…she's game all the time and sporty, a winner, a champion and she's witty.

H-istorian…her memory of the past, a lesson for the future, time traveler might she be, a teacher of wise lecture.

I-rresistible…as charming as she is now, as attractive as she'll be, her words of endearment is something one cannot flee.

J-oker…she has giggles and chuckles, on the way to laughing tracks, and crazy sense of humor, very funny jokes she cracks.

K-eeper…To her, one can depend on, secrets are only to her, she's someone worthy of trust not a gossip, not a murmur.

L-istener, Leader… a true born leader she is, straightforward, fearless host, and a powerful speaker, but a good listener at most.

M-other…not biologically, not a foster nor a step, she's a maternal figure, a genuine and an adept.

N-urse…, numerologist… a caregiver she is too; faultless nursing she has done, as good as her memory with numbers starting from one.

O-ptimist… she is one who never sulks for she always finds a way even when things reach a cram, she always brightens her day.

P-oet, psychologist…the words that flow from her mouth, are as witty as her brain with such love of making poems, there is something sure to gain.

Q-uestor… she is an adventurer, she exceeds her boundaries, she could separate the same and unite the contraries.

R-eader… the knowledge one gains from books, shows an image of her highness broadening mentality, a clear woman of prowess.

S-inger…when words turn into music, when her speech turns into a song, a beautiful melody, one is ought to sing along.

T-urtle lover…she's very fond of turtles, and turtles are fond of her, amazing person she is, as a mother of seven turtles.

U-ltimatum… a woman of principle, her first is always final, she sticks with her decision, no turns, no doubts, no denial.

V-irtuous…blameless in structure apart pure in mind, body and soul a woman of great virtue, her spirituality's whole.

W-riter…she does speak what she does write, she does write what she does speak, her mind's working both means, she is using it at its peak.

X-traordinaire…she is unpredictable, she is smart and she is slick, she's extraordinary her swift wits are really quick.

Y-outhfulness…these are the cherish moments, she is very young at heart, she patterns herself with age, enjoying her social part.

Z-oolander… a lover of animals, carrying an unmatched care, a giver of hope and life, rescuer of unaware.

By Francis John Angelo A. Jimenez

At first I was hesitant to share his alphabetical poem because it was too much of a description about me. I felt embarrassed. But I was appreciative of my nephew's inspiring notes. His poem added to feeding my soul. I was just one blessed aunt with my supportive and thoughtful nephew.

The truth was when I re-read the poem, I felt there was a life in me. I felt I was special. Part of my identity crisis was resolved. Let us admit, we liked to be praised, to be admired and to be liked. I have to admit that the good thing I have heard about me, made it easier for me to climb up- higher. It gave me strength. This is reality. When an ego is fed, the body became stronger and the strength gave me energy and the energy improved the process of healing. Climbing up high is a way to inner healing. The effort made by the people and with my own effort and the fervent prayers led me to climb up further. Again, the poem made me love myself more, and made me realized again that I am created in GOD's Image.

I felt I am worthy to live in this world and worthy to be loved by GOD and most of all worthy to be healed and worthy to serve mankind.

SELF-ANALYSIS

Analysis is something to do when you want to know the truth. It's like an investigation of what's going on within.

In other words I can analyze myself, examine myself, and investigate my inner self as to the whys, whats, when, where and the hows of everything.

The question I would like to ask myself is "Why Me?" Then, the next question I needed to ask is "Why Not Me?" I have mentioned earlier that Depression is a Blessing. My depression is the turning point of my life.

Not everyone is given the gift of courage and boldness to face the reality, to face the traumatic experience, and to face the past dim moments of our life. I was given such gift of courage. This book will testify on that brave heart of mine.

It took me a long deep breath before I started this special topic, my (not expected) confession. I have mentioned earlier the possible causes of my mental depression and through the 1:1 session, a lot of pertinent information revealed. But that time I could say I was ready to heed a most delicate self- confession after self-analysis. I never told this to anyone except to my mother on her death bed. I was crying and she was hugging me looking so frail and I was also shaking. I whispered the word "mother" in our dialect, and I said "Inay", I am sorry for whatever I've done to hurt you". "I want you to know that I love you and I will be missing you a lot". "Inay, I want to tell you something?" My mother was just stroking my hair and she hugged me tight and uttered, "What is it my child?" Then, I confessed to her that when I was five years old, three boys (our neighbors) molested me. They were between nine years old to eleven years old. I had been suppressing this uneasy feeling for a long, long time. I kept this to myself through out my self-awareness life. When my mother found out that terrible and horrible incident (during my childhood life) she cried and uttered, "My dear child I am very sorry for what had happened to you." When I looked at my mother's face, I felt her heart. I could feel that she was hurting too. And the thing that gave me goose bump was when she said, "Don't worry my dear daughter, I will take your heartaches and trauma in heaven with me. I will pray for your continuous inner healing".

I am just blessed that this dark part of my life didn't get worse. Most of the cases or most victims of molestation didn't survive the tragedy of shame, injustice and condemnation. As young as I was, I was innocently unbothered of what had happened. I couldn't remember if I cried or even told somebody about it. All I know now, I became aware of the reasons why I was manifesting some mental behaviors as depersonalization, anxiety end for sure even this dreadful illness as depression.

Upon knowing the possible causes of depersonalization in relation to identity crisis, I can conclude that whatever happened to my childhood life was a contributing factor in my own struggle.

In doing self-analysis you cannot fabricate information. Every information gathered is factual. I need indeed to analyze what was it that may have caused my depersonalization. It felt like I was putting myself under a lie detector or polygraph. I was indeed serious about analyzing myself, I would rather be honest with myself through self-analysis than being analyzed by somebody else.

What I was about to reveal in this analysis was partly a confession of my long time dark moments of my life. This shady life of mine was part of why I was suffering from depersonalization. (The key to secrecy of the dark area of my life was the "hidden trauma" that innocently surfaced) Something in the past and it was in my very remote memory that things happened. It was indeed a "blast from the past". I admit that if not for the gift of courage, I won't be able to include this traumatic incident in this book.

I believe that self-analysis is a way to rediscovery. My rediscovery of my self makes me more acquainted with myself, handles myself better and can protect myself from any threatening situation. The key to success of my recovery was my own self-analysis. While I was seeing my psychologist and psychiatrist, I was definitely doing my own self-analysis. My writing in my journal was a form of analyzing every situation I was in.

Getting to know myself is the best self-analysis. Part of my climbing up high is knowing myself. Myself is giving the whole direction in going up higher. So, I climbed up way up high.

A person who is suffering from a depression is like being imprisoned to his or her own cell, which they feel there's no way out. The only way out is through fervent prayers. This is what I called, "self-entrapment". I am being entrapped by my own fear, my strange feeling, and my identity crisis and my unexplainable emptiness that blocks my insight.

It is through imprisonment and seclusion that a person can have time to ponder and focus on oneself. In the gradual process, healing can take place, through thorough self-analysis.

It is difficult for a person to be imprisoned, especially those with a lifetime sentence. I could imagine the number of inmates who have been victims of D.A.D. (Depersonalization, Anxiety and Depression). To be in jail just for a month maybe irritating. Maybe for at least seven months, it is agonizing and maybe for a year it is already compromising and already getting accustomed to the cultural imprisonment.

It is between the prisoners and GOD. It is between the victims of depression and GOD. It takes fervent, unceasing prayers to the road of inner healing. Every moment spent in the prison is every moment chance for self-analysis and every moment chance to discover the road to soul's recovery.

LIFE GOES ON

Obladi! Oblada! Life goes on! Yes, that is the start of the song. How I wish we could easily start our life with obladi, oblada. The time that you can and will encounter the phrase "Life goes on" is the time when you would have been through any unpleasant experiences, relationship and untoward events.

When I was at the midst of my dim moments, I didn't have any plans for betterment, because I wasn't aware of the real essence of what was going on in my surroundings. I was just going on with the flow of whatever was flowing.

Life is a passive and an active movement. If you are well and healthy there goes the active part of your life. Then if you're ill, the caring is done by somebody or what we call second person, then there goes the passive move.

I didn't do any measures to get better, because I didn't know, I didn't want to and I didn't care at all. It killed my previous life. Now I am resurrected. This was my description of my negativity before.

Actually when I stopped smoking, when I took necessary vitamins, and my prescribed medicines, when I used my given talent (by our Creator) of writing books and paintings, when I started to write this particular book and ultimately when I sang obladi,-oblada, then I moved on, so my life went on and still going on.

The bottom line is which I should say since the beginning.

Prayer is the answer
Prayer is there, it never failed me
Prayer is my forever, companion

Prayer taught me a lot
Prayer is a friend to talk to
Prayer is the bridge between me and the Almighty
Prayer is a heart beat away.

And our GOD is the sole owner of Prayer and the Great Listener.

How could I not get well?
How could I ignore the essence of life?
How could I forget my Almighty's existence?

And yes I need to share without inhibitions that I am A Depression Survivor.

Obladi, oblada, Life Goes On!

When a relationship is broken, you will hear this "phrase" "Move on". Of course we expect for that person to follow such phrase. Moving on should undergo a process. You can not do it in one week to be healed and whatever length of time for that matter.

It is different when you are suffering from D. A. D. (Depersonalization, Anxiety and Depression.) It's a long way to get better. It's a long process to find the inner healing and it's a high peak to climb. This is the peak of peace, healing and normalcy. It is true whatever happens in **our life, life goes on.**

Life Goes On is a very powerful phrase
Life Goes On is a motivation to follow through
Life Goes On is an inspiration to look forward to
Life Goes On is a model of positivity
Life Goes On is a guide to follow to avoid the crooked way
Life Goes On is a way that the heartbroken walk through
Life Goes On is the initial approach and ultimate goal for life's betterment

If I didn't believe in this phrase "Life Goes On", I won't be able to even give importance to this phrase; I won't be able to write books; and I won't be able to think of climbing up to reach my goal. Yes, life is too short, yet Life Goes On.

Esther Jimenez

It is true that we should not count the number of times we fall, it is important that we acknowledge the number of times we get up. Getting up is just like climbing up but the difference is in climbing up you could still climb up higher. Whether you are getting up or climbing up the bottom line is "LIFE GOES ON".

Climb Up Way Up High

TOTAL SHIFT

A shifting is a change of something. It can be from no to yes. It can be from negative to positive. It is also a change of direction from left to right.

The total shift I am referring to, is the magic book. The mystery book that is used to be blank, yet it welcomes anybody to fill it up. Then you can flip the time of event from yesterday to today. It is a shift from nothing to something.

That is the old testimony of my life. The new testimony of my life is the transformation of my life, the total shift of the magic book. Journaling is one of the instruments for my recovery. It did help me a lot, pouring out everything in that journal book. It is a road, it's like a gross forest, or a thorny ground, plus getting inside the dark cave or endless tunnel. These are the views you will see inside my journal. You can't see the exit. But there was a whole within and that was the window for the new testimony book.

I see the gradual and the slow motion movement of the changes of the story of my Depression. With the gifts of the Holy Spirit the talents I have and the multiplicity of handling these talents I am very thankful. The new testimony of my life transformation, was changed to writing more. I was so inspired and it was overwhelming feeling, thoughts, words, and virtues were coming out from my mouth and heart.

I started writing almost everyday since I unwrapped my gifts. I always tell the people I have encountered, that all of us were given gifts by the Holy Spirit. All we have to do is to unwrap it. In my case, I did.

My journal book was full of positive thoughts since then. To my surprise, I was able to write my first book, 365 Days Food For Thoughts. It was not from a publishing company, but I was happy. I had it printed by a regular printing press. The next was the "Bible Tidbits" my very first book from a publishing company. In between my writing, I discover my ability to paint using brush and canvasses (from mini- canvass to a big canvass.) Not only that, I started picking up stones (from pebbles to garden stones and I made them beautiful as I was painting them.)

And this was another total shift, from blank stones to colorful ones. So I accomplished something that is making use of the talents I received.

I continued writing and the second book was "What's In My Heart?" volume I and the third was the volume II of "What's In My Heart?" So in the span of fourteen years I published eight books totally. As I am writing this, I do proudly present this ninth book, "CLIMB UP WAY UP HIGH"

Now I am sharing all these not to brag about my accomplishment but to let you know the transformation of the journal book. This is the total shift of recovery.

In my climbing up I have used a lot of strong carbiners, quickdraws and harness (these are rock climbers lingo.) These were my supportive objects. I was closed to the peak through the gifts of the Holy Spirit. Climb up! Way Up High! I am up now. These carbiners, quickdraws and harness were my spiritual allies.

Sometimes we do things seemed crazy yet we still do it. We do it because of some weird reasons. One reason might be a *dare game or a being challenged game.*

But whatever the reasons are, the key is doing the odd things voluntarily or involuntarily. What about the real situation wherein a prompt from the Holy Spirit, that you need to do something unpsychological yet somebody will benefit from doing it. A typical example is preaching along the street, claiming your belief. For most people this doing is crazy. And for some, this is a way of proselytizing. But for them it is not. They were just doing it because they were led to do it.

How about what happened to me? I was manifesting anxiety, sometimes panic attack? I might looked crazy or something was wrong, but in the mind of my loved ones my condition is **treatable**. And yes, it is **treatable.** What do you call this? I called this a total shift from hopeless case to a surviving soul. *I am here, am I not?*

This chapter is a little bit confusing. I intentionally wrote this to let you feel a part of me when I was confused. A total shift is a Blessing. A total shift is a transformation. A total shift is Climbing Up Way Up High!

"Hope" is the key to a total shift. The support and love of the family brings hope for a total recovery. It is very essential to have hope. A hopeless and helpless depressed human being can be shifted to a hopeful and enthusiastic being. This is the meaning of a total shift. I believed that in any kind of mental illness, there's always a chance to attain the inner healing.

With the fervent prayers of those who are supporting me and with my strong will to get better and get healed, and with the treatment and measures I utilized, I felt the total shift of everything. I got better, I recovered and I was healed and conquered my D.A.D. (Depersonalization, Anxiety and Depression) challenges. I climbed up indeed way up high and proud to claim "I am a Depression Survivor". I was willing to get help and I had it. I was willing to change and I got better. I was willing to enter a total shift, and I survived.

My brother (the one next to me) once told me, everytime he hears the song "Climb Every Mountain" he is reminded him of ME. If he believed I can climb to survive, he is absolutely right. So join me in my journey, let us climb up together. Let us shift direction in a positive way and let's climb up way up high.

PSYCHOLOGICAL PAIN

Is there such a psychological pain? How does a mind gets hurt?

My psychologist once told me that "psychological pain" is more painful than physical pain. I didn't realize that I was already manifesting psychological pain.

At first I didn't understand the meaning of that. How can I compare the pain that time when in fact I didn't even care what was going on in my life and in my surroundings.

Now I realized there's truth in what my psychologist had told me. I have found out through the years the different scenarios or instances, and different kinds of weird stories coming out from the people's anxious minds.

I heard from somebody how her sister behaved when attacked by the planet Anxiety. She said, she felt like there was a thunder in her heart. And she would like to run fast but she couldn't move.

When I was a mental health counselor we had this group session, and one of the clients verbalized his feelings and his voice was pitchy. He described his thoughts as, as if there was a sharp-edge pain into his mind cutting him and radiating through his spine.

She said something like, "feeling falling from the small carriage or wagon like and something was pushing her on her side, yet pulling her too". And this occurred on her mind on and off. She was holding her head and covering her ears. I guessed that there were more stories, more testimonies, more incidents that I have not witnessed nor heard yet, and they are just around the corner. How about the next eventful story, are you ready?

I have experienced different painful thoughts. One of them was I felt tightness on my head, from frontal to both of my parietal sides of my head. I felt a wide rubber band tied into my head. And I felt empty inside my head, but I felt the vacuum covering the linings of my skull.

When I was seven years old, my father told me that he was pulling me out of the small space. I was under our small size dresser. We didn't know if that was because I was convulsive. It so happened that I was running very high temperature. Whether from fever or an impending episode of my anxiety, it didn't matter that time. It matters to me now, because I didn't realize it would be significant and impactful to my life at present time. But one thing sure was, there was another information that I would like to reveal.

This revelation happened when I was five years old. It might look like there was no relevance to any of the topics we're talking about, but mind you there was, especially with anxiety.

I was walking in my sleep that early age. It is called *"somnambulism"*. I have discovered that in one of the brochures I read regarding "somnambulism", was that children of all ages are not exempted from anxiety. So my sleep walking had something to do with my anxiety. In other words sleep walking and anxiety are relevant.

There were three occasions that I could still remember about my sleepwalking. In one occasion I was sleep walking and went to the restaurant near by (few houses from our house). And I was asking for an ice cream in a cone. While I was eating my ice cream, I was pulling down the little banners hanging by the ceiling within my reach. I didn't know that my aunt followed me and slowly assisted me in going back home.

Again another sleep walking episode happened and it almost cost my life. This happened when we were still at the same old house. We used to live near a railroad track, actually near the restaurant where I had my first sleep walking episode. So I was sleep walking again. This time nobody noticed that I was walking towards the door, until I reached the side street pavement by the railroad track. I was hearing voices of men at the corner store seemed having a drinking session. There was a train coming. I didn't hear the tsug! tsug! tsug!

sound, but I felt a grab on my left arm. It was one of the guys in the corner store. He saved my life. He was not drunk after all. He saved a five year old "somnambulist" girl.

Again, when I reached my seventh year, another sleeping walking episode happened. This one was something funny. When we moved to a new house, of course there was a lot of adjustment in my surroundings for all of us. I knew I was anxious, but not aware I supposed, (because I was only a child.) So I guessed my anxiety was caused by adjustment of moving to a new house. So the funny thing was, I was sleep walking again and while my father was sleeping I poured out a bedpan of urine on him. Good thing it was not on his face, it was just on the lower limbs. He didn't get mad because he knew about my sleep walking problem. The thing was I managed to carry a round made of enamel bedpan with handle like a pail so it was easier, to carry. This was not like the flat hospital bedpan. That's why a seven year old girl can manage to carry it. *Ironic but funny.*

After relating to you my semi-dim childhood life, I know that you would and could understand more about why and how I suffered from Depersonalization, Anxiety and Depression. I can testify now that psychological pain is more painful than physical pain. In climbing up high, way up high, there will be encounters before you can reach the top. The truth was I didn't feel much of the psychological pain because I was only a child. If I did, I did not understand what it was. But if somebody would ask me, how the pain was, during the later years, I would have the answers for that somebody. The pain was indescribable and it was beyond grasp. This was one of the challenges and one of the plights I fought for.

I will continue climbing up, way up high to defeat my own D.A.D. (Depersonalization, Anxiety and Depression) Challenge.

DISABILITY

I never thought that disability has a great impact with the normalcy in life. I remember we have an elementary song in our dialect (Tagalog) that describes the "Ten Fingers and Toes", the face with two eyes, two ears, clean teeth, beautiful nose, etc. This is describing a complete body parts. To my countrymen: for sure you know this elementary song, entitled, "Sampung Mga Daliri" What I am trying to emphasize here is how to function without restrictions. But we have to realize that we don't have any control in our life's situation. We can only be watchful, careful and be aware of our surroundings and the things we are doing. By doing these we can avoid accidents to happen, also sickness, poverty, loss and other mishaps in life that can contribute to the interruptions of the normality of life.

I included disability as part of the topic in my book because I want to tackle the relevance of disability to my own disability. What is a disability anyway? It is a condition that restricts the activities of a person because of certain impairment. That impairment restricts the normal functioning of an individual. That's the reason why an individual with disability acquires a handicap sticker for the car. The most common disabilities are with restrictions in walking, talking, especially the ones in wheelchairs. Others are with brain injury or with Chronic Depression.

I have a handicap sticker that I used in my car. Why do I attain one? I don't have a problem in walking and I don't use wheelchair in going to regular stores or to any of my appointments. I must admit I am using wheelchair in traveling like the (airport's wheelchair.) I couldn't walk that long anymore. And my handicap sticker was with me since I was diagnosed with depression. Now, the more I need the handicap sticker for my physical restricted activities, because I am already 3/4 of a century and cannot walk properly, and sometimes I was out of balance. Let me just share this significant job history that is relevant to my acquiring disability privileges. I have mentioned earlier that I had a long list of resume. I didn't have an impressive resume at all. How I became a candidate for disability benefit recipient? Here is the story.

Since I was not working full time nor have a stable job at all, I thought of trying to apply for disability. And since I didn't know much about it, I asked a lawyer that was recommended by one of my friends, to help me. I started submitting the required documents as medical proof of my seeing a psychiatrist and a psychologist, (in other words my medical records), my job history, my income tax return and even my educational attainment. After I have submitted the requirements I just waited for the approval. Many applicants that I have talked to, told me that there were many applicants that were being denied. Some were denied not only once but three to four times. To be honest I was not really gung ho whether I would be approved or not. Maybe because I was still very depressed and I had no interest in what's going on. But I needed to go on, right? Que sera, sera, obladi, oblada, (whatever will be, will be, life goes on)

After four months, I was surprised when I received a letter from the office of the Social Security (attorneys' office) that I was approved and in three months time I would start receiving $ 670.00 monthly. And I received certain amount of money as initial benefit payment and only for one time. To be honest I couldn't remember how much was that amount. I had a mixed feeling that time when I received that letter. I was glad that I would be able to receive something monthly, yet I had self-pity knowing that I could be living a normal nurse salary wage, but it didn't happen. The thing that made me cry was the contents of the letter from the lawyer's office from the Social Security office. I can't tell you word for word but I can tell you the emotional impact in me. The lawyer said that,"*a nurse like her could have earned a better salary if she can work in a normal capacity, and with her very high education, she should be receiving the money she desired. And because of her mental condition it restricts her in receiving the proper amount as a nurse wage. So no need for court hearing, hence, she should and would be granted approval."* So the mixed feelings I had were glad and sad (with additional self-pity.) I was very appreciative of the approved benefits. So, it's only logic to conclude that my career as a nurse has gone with the wind; the wind that swept away by the depersonalization, anxiety and depression.

Let us clear these things out. Physical disability is tantamount to mental disability. I have a very beautiful poem for the blessed handicap beings. I honor and respect them.

BLESSED ARE THE HANDICAPS

*Let's pause for a moment and ponder on
the thoughts of how lucky we are
to have a thought process.
Now, let's imagine a person who can't see
blind totally, those who can't speak and
can't talk, or those with difficulty of speech.
How about the deaf, who can't hear and
those who who can't walk, or no limbs at all
And yet, there are those who can hear, can talk
can see and walk, but no insights at all,
Their insights were stolen by severe
depression, drugs, narcotics and alcohol,
mentally handicaps are the mentally retarded
and (what they call mentally challenge) and
mentally-ill.
So, aren't we lucky we can hear, talk, see
and walk?
Not so! Not so! Not so!
For there are some people who can do
anything and everything, but they lack the
essence of compassion.
So let's be content, with what we have
We are lucky, but handicaps are blessed.
They are mentors in our spirituality.
GOD loves them and blesses them all.*

We are handicaps too, in some points
But we are recipients of GOD's graces
So cheers to all, including the handicaps,
Let's rejoice for we are all created in GOD'S
IMAGE.

There is no hindrance in climbing up high, whether a disable or a handicap, it doesn't matter. I used my mental disability as a challenge to reach the normalcy, normality to the full capacity. If they can do it, I can do it. If I can do it, they can do it. So let us climb up high way up high. Many sports celebrities, even ordinary souls who have disabilities can reach the topmost, the finish line with flying colors and smiles on their faces. Winners don't quit and climbers never give up. I am a climber of D.A.D challenge (Depersonalization, Anxiety and Depression.)

Climb Up Way Up High

SUICIDAL THOUGHTS

Suicidal thought is one of the symptoms of depression. Suicide is one of the leading causes of death in the United States. What exactly is suicide? It is defined as death caused by self-directed injurious behavior with intent to die as a result of the behavior. Not only ordinary people commit suicide. Even the popular people like the celebrities are victims too. Suicide is not selective. It could victimized everyone who are involved in an everyday encounter in life. But very rare in children, more in young ones (youth).

One time I noticed a big frame poster in the clinic where my psychiatrist office was. It was a frame consisted of names of celebrities who suffered from Depression and at least three of them died of committing suicide. That was the year 2000, so almost two decades ago. Whatever the numbers were, maybe this time the numbers were doubled.

Just recently a famous chef died, he committed suicide. A teenager celebrity in our country also committed suicide last year. I didn't have any right to give advice especially if I was just expressing my inner thoughts regarding teenage suicides. I am only basing my sharing through my own inner thoughts about it. I have been there and I could save somebody through knowing what I have been through, maybe someone might find some relief of mutual experience thing. *All I can say is, let us be watchful for the signs of wanting to reach out. Always be mindful of the changing behaviors and words coming out from their mouth. Let us be extra sensitive, my dear parents.*

Depression like I said is ***treatable***. If we treat the depression right, we are preventing suicide episode. Let us be aware of the victims of mental illness, especially major depression. Mental pain is important as any physical pain and discomfort.

I never seriously attempted to commit suicide. As I have mentioned in my previous page that I have some suicidal thoughts, but not seriously thinking of actually doing it. Because of the unbearable psychological pain, many unpleasant thoughts were playing in my mind.

Let me share with you a glimpse of my dim moments regarding suicidal thoughts. Sometimes I want to give up. Here are some of the phrases I uttered during my hopeless moments; "I can't stand it", "I want to disappear." Literally, I meant that. But I cannot even fathom the possible outcome. That was exactly my fear. I was scared of what would happen after I did it. I couldn't understand what was happening with my thoughts. But I was certain with the uncertainty of feeling empty headed. Every time I had that kind of attack, I was holding my rosary inside my pocket tightly. I feel safe by just holding it.

Maybe for those who had the same experience of uncertainty like mine couldn't stand anymore and couldn't think of any measures to overcome the attack. And maybe after frequent attack they panic and resorted to killing themselves. It is important to *pray, (no need of a long one)*. Repeatedly pray for mercy to get well and I did this. I prayed even though I didn't know the essence of what I was praying that time, and because of the uncertainties that I was feeling. GOD feels every bit of what a person is saying. For me He was, He is and He will be my utmost, highest and mightiest power.

For those who are aware of the Twelve Steps in AA, they are referring to the word, "highest" power. Yes, the Highest Power, the Source of Healing. My highest power is the LORD JESUS. And I asked His Mother Blessed Virgin Mary to intercede for me and with me.

*Un*pleasant thoughts, *un*certainties are *un*called for. I am a victim of this "*un*". But I thought of GOD's *un*conditional love and *un*limited blessings, so I was able to survive through *un*doing my thoughts from negative to positive things. **It takes a 100% surrender and trust to the highest power and a 0% to our doubts.**

Again, my climbing up way up high helped me a lot in undoing these unpleasant thoughts. We cannot ignore the increase rates of suicides. Let us fervently pray for the victims.

HOW TO SUPPORT VICTIMS OF SUICIDES?

S-incerity is needed when talking to the victims of suicides
U-nderstanding is recommended for better recovery
I-ntervention is important, but carry it cautiously
C-aring, courage and commitment must be carefully given
I-ntercede with humility and offer fervent prayers
D-elicately handle the victims and remove threatening objects.
E-ncourage to verbalize more and engage in positive conversation

LIFE IS TOO SHORT; LET'S NOT MAKE IT SHORTER. LOVE YOURSELF, FOR YOU ARE CREATED IN GOD'S IMAGE.

PSYCHODYNAMICS

Not everybody knows the meaning of psychodynamics. But people in the medical field understands the meaning of this term, especially in the field of psychiatry.

I am a nurse and I learned the word, "psychodynamics" when I was in Nursing and it was a part of the Psychiatric Nursing subject.

Psychodynamics is the psychology of mental, behavioral or emotional forces or processes developing especially in early childhood and their effects on behavior or mental states. It explains or interprets its status.

In simple explanation "psychodynamics" is how a child is being brought up. Yes, the upbringing of children. The growing up of the children go through different stages. Actually, all of us goes to the different stages of life, and they called it developmental stages. We are not going into details here. We will just talk about the relationship of ones behavior with growing up. I am sure you are familiar with the saying, "Like father, like son." There is truth in this. That's when the psychodynamics enter. The genes, DNA, the ways and mannerisms are responsible for the similarities of the father and son What if the son was just adopted? How the son was brought up had something to do with the behavior he was showing. It is just like a profiling system to know more of the individual.

My father was a nervous type but not my mother. And I was the same as my father. Part of my psychodynamics was my hereditary line. Obviously I got my history of nervous breakdown from the genes that composed my body.

From one incident after another incident, I found out that my uncle committed suicide. I did not witness the actual sight of the place where he did it, but I still saw the rope hanging. We were not blood related (he was the husband of my aunt,)(the sister of my mother), in short her brother– in –law). This incident is worth to mention because it was a traumatic experienced that contributed to my childhood like. It is part of my psychodynamics. I was four and a half years old then. I gathered an information from my psychiatrist that such sight of the rope hanging contributed to my mental aspect of growing up. That was not a good memory. Little that I have heard or seen during the funeral, I still could feel the tension of the incident.

This is part of my psychodynamics, (environment.) The mini incidents (the traumatic ones) are part of my psychodynamics. Sometimes those memories that are in the subconscious minds are the ones in the later years. There are memories that can make us smile and memories that can ruin our day, even future life. That was my preschool stage of child development.

My mother was telling me that the night before I was born, November 23, the year 1947, they (she and my father) went to see a movie, "Gone With The Wind". *No wonder I am sweet.* That was a romantic movie. The movie had no bearing with my being sweet. Before midnight my mother was having abdominal contractions. After the movie they went directly to the hospital. Thirty minutes after midnight there was a baby girl born, can't remember the weight (in which my mother told me), as long as it was in normal range. Yes, "A Star Was Born" on November 24,1947. Not intentionally given but the name given was *Estrella (meaning Star in Spanish)*. So there came A Star.

My infancy stage started pretty good. I was the oldest among all the siblings, (including among my cousins on both mother and father sides.) The reason I emphasized that, was, being the oldest grandchild, I got all the attention from the elders. No wonder I grew up feeling loved by my aunts, uncles, my grandmother and grandfather (aunt and uncle of my mother.) There was a big smile on my face every time my mother told me the story about my grandmother and grandfather used to pick me up early morning and returned me home late at night. Since I didn't witness the exact pleasant story, I still felt their strong love and care through my mother's bedtime story or mother-daughter bonding time.

I spent the five years of my life in a quite bad neighborhood closed to a railroad track. When we moved to the new house I was already almost seven years old. I did not know then the significance of adjustment, but I knew it had something to do with my psychodynamics.

My first attack of "depersonalization" was when I was seven years old. I already mentioned this particular incident in the first chapter "WHO AM I? I am mentioning it again in this chapter as part of my psychodynamics.

One great merit part of my school age was I received a third honor diploma when I was on my first grade. As a seven year old girl with an early challenge in life, at least there was a reward at the same stage of my life.

I am glad that I can still recall the important events in my life that can help me in this sharing of my private life, and to contribute in relating the history of my triad mental illness, (Depersonalization, Anxiety and Depression.)

When I was nine years old my mother was hospitalized at the Lung Hospital because she developed this progressive lesion in one of her ribs. This was caused by accidental puncture on the right side of her torso and penetrated her rib cage, during Japanese war. She underwent surgery. She was hospitalized for almost three years. It took that long because of other serious complications. So, no mother figure around. I remember that once a month, and that was every weekend, we were visiting our mother at the Philippine Lung Hospital. Every time we visited her I would always cry, because I knew I was going to miss her right after visiting hour was over. See I was the oldest among the siblings, she would start saying her caring litany lists for me to follow. She would give me instructions on taking care of my younger siblings. I was only between ten to eleven years of age, but I felt like a sixteen year old responsible girl. That's one of the reasons I was tomboyish, trying to discipline my siblings. Not only that I was disciplining them but I also had time playing with them.

That time, me and my two brothers were transferred to a public school. I couldn't forget my first day of school. I was elected "president of the council just in our section. I think they were impressed when I was asked to recite the "Pledge of Allegiance. We didn't have it from the school I came from. So in other words I was able to memorize the Pledge of Allegiance in fifteen minutes. At the end of the school year I was given an award (a diploma certificate) as one of the Ten Outstanding Elementary Students. I would never forget the gift of my mother gave me. It was a Bulova wrist watch (still a brand name) at present time. Actually it was hers and she just gave to me. My mother was crying when she pinned the medal on my left lapel and I felt that she was proud of me. My elementary years were over and there was a tinge (pinch) in my heart knowing I would be missing my classmates and teachers. Good-bye E.S.E.S. (Epifanio delos Santos Elementary School.)

High school years were also memorable. I didn't have "depersonalization" attack. But I have figured out that four years of schooling were enough gauge as to where my "identity crisis" rooted. As a teenager I encountered these crushes and avoiding few suitors that were circling around. At the same time there were classmates and batchmates who were sending me love notes. That's why I was a little bit confused, questioning myself about those love notes, because they came from my female classmates/batchmates. The funny thing was my father found those letters hidden in between my folded clothes. He didn't even get mad. I realized that I had an understanding and loving father.

Academically speaking, I didn't have honor when I graduated, but I was in a high section when I graduated. Being in a high section meant a lot because high section would be seen marching first on the line on graduation day. Even without any honor, I still had received some merits. I was chosen to be a directress in one of the plays we presented. I can't forget the name of that play, "Merchant of Venice" by William Shakespeare. It was a successful play.

Earlier I have mentioned about my Pre-Nursing school life that included my being a working student. Let us jump up to my three year internship life, living in a dormitory with about 35 to 40 ladies boarding. We had two matrons (taking care of our welfare and of course including disciplining us.) I enjoyed my nursing life, the fact that I loved to be a nurse. As long as I live, I will treasure my nursing moments (my Florence Nightingale memories.)

During my Nursing internship I had few suitors and committed to at least three boyfriends not at the same time though, but one at a time. I didn't do much of dating because of the dormitory restrictions. But the weird thing was I also committed to few girlfriends. Will this be the one of the causes of my "identity crisis"? It was getting clearer that part of me was displaying another personality. Again and let me reiterate, I didn't have split personality. I was just expressing who I was. And maybe because of the environment exposure to a majority of women? As long as I didn't harm anybody or hurting somebody, I wouldn't feel guilty of my being me.

That was another measure I needed to remember, a clear conscience to face GOD and people. Guilt feelings is one of the causes of depersonalization, inhibition of who a person really was? Whatever I shared in this book was based on my experiences and encounters. And if ever I mentioned some of the bits and pieces of my life, they were contributing factors that made the person that I was and the person that I am. This is still part of my psychodynamics.

I didn't have a scholastic honor during my internship, but I was nominated as "Child of Mary". Since the school name was Marian School of Nursing, every year there was a model for being Child of Mary. We were five nominees, but my classmate from Ilocos region got it. She was a daughter of a Pastor and she belonged to a very big nice family. For me, I was glad and appreciative of just being nominated. I found out that one of our clinical instructors (our clinical instructor in Psychiatric Nursing) was the one who nominated me. When I got the chance to talk to her, she told me that she knew my father when she was a student in a reputable nursing school and when she was at the dormitory she happened to see my father delivering letters in the hospital where my father was working. Her comment was, my father was a gentleman, courteous and obedient person like me, so "like father, like daughter". There goes my progressive psychodynamics.

After my internship, I landed a job at the institution where I graduated. I worked as a pioneer ICU nurse. Part of my life experience were already shared in my previous confession. This psychodynamics of mine is taking too long because of the length of how I am living in this world. The more I aged the longer my story is. Actually, a psychodynamics is just an autobiography of ones behavior and who I was and who I am. It is about the contributing factors affecting my personality.

I just celebrated my 70th birthday last November 24, 2017 and proud to share my gifts given by our Almighty, the gift of painting and the gift of writing books. Not bad for a seventy year old lady still able to appreciate the beauty of the world.

Part of my adulthood psychodynamics were already mentioned in the previous chapters. I am now almost at the end of my story and towards the Epilogue. The climbing is not over. Challenges are always facing me and climbing has always helped me in focusing on getting healed. Healing is the best result that a climber like me can ever be grateful for, thankful for and appreciative of, through my entire life. Again, climbing up way up high made me feel empowered.

Climb Up Way Up High

SUPPORT OF THE FAMILY AND FRIENDS

If at the beginning of my depression ordeal, I didn't have my family to support me, I would have ended in a psychiatric facility or ended up dead. I sounded morbid, but it is the truth.

Support of the family and friends is an important factor in dealing with the depersonalization, anxiety and depression. The family and friends are considered the wall that we can lean on, when we are down and needed a support (physically, emotionally and even psychologically.) GOD is our strength and He gave the family as the additional strength.

I still believed that, "no man is an island". That's the reason GOD created Eve so that Adam can have a companion even in the beginning of creation. ***GOD thought of a family support even then.***

I mentioned earlier that the support of the family and friends is very essential to road to recovery. It is one of the keys to a successful therapy. Where there is support, there must be compassion. I have felt the love, caring, compassion and warmth of my family and close friends. My father was the one who recognized that I needed help. He approached me gently and asked me if I wanted to see a psychiatrist. My mother was very caring, not only in words but in deeds. She was rubbing my back with vicks vaporub and sometimes talcum powder to give soothing effect for my whole body. She was always aware of how I was feeling, what I was feeling and always ready to make me feel comfortable and calm. It felt like there was a big baby at home. My cousin who witnessed all my anxiety attacks and bouts of depersonalization and dim moments of depression was always trying to calm me down, holding my hands, offering water or juice to soothe my dry throat and anything that would pacify me. Since most of the members of my family were in our country, the Philippines, they were trying to extend their love and warmth through overseas calls and sending me cards and letters to cheer me up. My brother who was staying in other States gave effort to visit me through long driving.

My friends visited me, brought me goods, offered group prayers even offering a healing mass and individual fervent prayers. Friends who couldn't come to visit were offering to lit candles for my fast recovery. Me, myself strongly believed in offering candles. I am doing this now. I have a candle lit in my altar continuously a votive offering for our Blessed Virgin Mother Mary. As a devoted Catholic, I solemnly offered my prayers with lit candles for anything that I am praying for.

One thing that I was grateful for was, not only the amazing love, caring, warmth, and compassion that I received from my family and friends, BUT the absence of condemnation, judgment and blame. Nobody condemned me, nor judged me and nor blamed me for whatever happened to me. THIS IS THE REAL MEANING OF SUPPORT.

It was like I just walked in a muddy ground that I could hardly walk. So when I was rescued, no one blame me nor the muddy ground, except they try to dry the ground for me to walk back to a plain smooth pathway.

Even some of my close friends who had gone ahead of me, who witnessed my dim journey, were very supportive in their own little sweet ways. I know you guys are in heaven now. Thank you for your love.

I consider the pets and some animals to be friends too. Our two cats and two dogs and favorite turtle named "PONG" who passed away played a big part in my getting better. Now we have a dog a Shih Tzu named, "BENJIE" and few turtles who are giving me joy and delight.

Compassion is the common denominator of all this relationship. I have a poem for all of us that will remind us that without compassion the support is not that strong and not that effective.

COMPASSION

A genuine heart must you possess
To tame an angry human being
A soft touch with caring thoughts
And with a tender, loving care
Compassion, a beautiful virtue to aim
You can start now and learn from it
It's an amulet for a raging bull
And a shield to protect you with.
With caring hand and a smiling face
With friendly gesture and shaking hands
With gentle words to the listening ears
And that is the meaning of compassion.
So be compassionate and be friendly
You will see the big change yourself
You didn't change the people,
You changed yourself
You changed the world, that is compassion.

Support must be continuously rendered for a better recovery. Support is not only a one word but meaningful seven letter word.

S-ave as many poor souls from the dungeon of depression
U-nderstanding the victims of mental illness and extend your help
P-roper treatment are needed to handle the mentally-ill, depressed individual
P-repare the victims to go back to the normality of life
O-ffer your sincere love and service to the depressed person
R-ender your utmost help with love and understanding
T-otally surrender everything to our GOD Almighty

Every support that is received is a step up in climbing. The more support I have, the higher I climb.

THE FINAL CURTAIN

Yes, the end of my rope of desperation is near. The struggle to face the mirror of deceit is diminishing. The earthquake that engulfs the delicate body of my being is starting to calm down, the anxiety slowly leaving and most of all the depression is pressed out and won't be allowed to sprout again. This is how to approach the losing battle, the battle of D.A.D.'s challenge. (Depersonalization, Anxiety and Depression)

It's a great feeling that I was able to overcome the bits and pieces of the dim moments. I didn't expect that I would be wanting to write a book about me, myself and my depression. I am a private person and very few or maybe only three to four people knew about my private life.

Things happen for a reason. And GOD Has plan for everyone. And being a victim of depersonalization that early age was a very unique case. Imagine after sixty three years of my life I am (still) fighting, fulfilling GOD's plan. I am seventy years old now. I was seven years old when my first episode of depersonalization happened. So, mathematically speaking, for sixty three years I have been going with the flow of my life as it has been my fate that those things happened.

Sometimes things aren't the ones we expect to happen yet it did happen. My whole life is an unexpected miracle. Unexpected is the mystery of "why me"? Expected is the recipient of multiple gratitude. I am just overwhelmed with the over power of GOD's love.

To be honest, I am now almost at the end of my manuscript, that's why I named this chapter "The Final Curtain". But I couldn't end it, because there are some loop-holes in my story but I can't pinpoint what. I will continue to write until I reach the stop sign.

Before I finally close the final curtain, let us explore what's in the dark area of the long years of suffering from a D.A.D. (Depersonalization, Anxiety and Depression.) All I could say is, we should not be afraid of the *dark*. We should be afraid what's in the *dark*. That's right! *Dark* is just a black color. It's just like when you close your eyes, you see nothing. So if you see nothing, nothing to be afraid of.

The next question is what's in the *dark?* Or what are in the *dark*? Whatever is in the *dark* or are in the *dark* indeed are the dim moments. The dim moments are my traumatic experiences, as in the depersonalization, anxiety and depression attacks; the trials that I have been through, the struggles that I learned to crawl through and the plight that I managed to fight with. They are my bumpy journey, the turbulence that I passed-by and the craters that I managed to evade because of climbing the steps of survivors. The final curtain isn't indeed the final. It is an opening to an enlightenment of more insights, blessings and life worth giving.

Meantime allow me to continue conversing with you. I am talking to my mind and my heart and I am reflecting on anything that would benefit every concerned citizens and curious readers.

One thing I noticed during my struggle was, "guilt" feelings. Guilt feelings played an important role in our everyday encounters. But there is one thing I learned regarding this… that do not dwell on guilt feelings. Instead of feeling guilty all the time, I prayed about it and ignore it. Clear conscience promotes clear thoughts and clear thoughts will attain more insights.

I am more grateful of the virtues I have cultivated in my life. So virtues, prayers, interactions and hopes were my weapons for the D.A.D. (Depersonalization, Anxiety and Depression) a challenge battle. I am well now and proudly say, my name is Esther B. Jimenez a Depression survivor.

I climbed up, way up high. My curtain of uncertainties is closed now but my curtain of hope is still widely open. So I'll continue my climbing up high way up high!

THE BEAUTY OF WORDS

As I have mentioned in the chapter before this, "The Final Curtain," I was hesitant to have a closure, because I could still feel I needed to say something. There it goes something popped up from my exploring mind.

I thought of gathering the poems that are excerpts from my two published books, "What's In My Heart? Volume I and Volume II. I chose the ones relevant to everything significant to the content of "CLIMB UP WAY UP HIGH". The first poem that I would like to share is about the totality of being me and my gratitude to everything and everybody.

SEE THROUGH MY SOUL

I see the beauty of life when
I wake up in the morning
I see hope when I look up the sky
I see the miracle of life when
I look at the mirror
Yes, you can see my true self
Through my soul
I see us the people of many faces
I see the wonderful talents in each one
I see how beautiful we are created in GOD's Image
Indeed I am thankful for my sight
And all my senses
I am grateful for all my blessings and graces

I am pleased with the loving
Family and great friends
You can see through my soul the
Fullness of my gratitude
Yes, GOD can see me through my
Very Being, through my SOUL.

I can't thank you enough for the support of my family and friends. You my loved ones, witnessed what I have been through, how I struggle and what I felt throughout. And my only hope and ultimate aid was my only LORD. I begged for His love and mercy. When a heart struggles, every part of your being struggles too.

MY STRUGGLING HEART

My heart speaks out of gripes and pains. My heart craves for consoling words
My heart strives for an utmost peace, Yes, I do have a struggling heart
I ask GOD to see my heart, I beg Him to feel my pain
I seek for His mercy and love, I want Him to touch my struggling heart.
LORD, this I beg of You to give
…fill my heart with Your wisdom
…fill my heart with humility
…fill my heart with Your love and mercy
…fill my heart with serenity
…fill my heart with understanding
…fill my heart with forgiveness
…fill my heart with inner healing
…fill my heart with peace
Yes my LORD fill me, my whole being with holiness and worthiness
Fill my heart with tranquility which my heart longs to receive and this heart is Yours to keep.

Like I said in the previous chapters that "psychological pain" is more painful than physical pain. I struggled so much battling with my thoughts. But it was my heart that struggled. And I did ask GOD to fill my heart with His love and mercy. But the utmost things I needed to be filled with is, to fill my heart with the Inner Healing.

The next poem is quite long. I think this is one of the longest poems I've written. The title is The Inner Healing. This is for all of us.

THE INNER HEALING

The world is a chaos.
The people are struggling.
The situation is overwhelming.
Where is the Inner Healing?
Animosity in the workplace
Relationship misunderstood
Burden is so heavy
Where is the Inner Healing?
The church is empty
The mall is full pack
The streets are crowded
Where is the Inner Healing?
Terrible, terminal illness
Hopeless case, helplessness
Craving for relief
Where is the Inner Healing?
Discrimination exists
Communication gap interferes
Humiliation surfaces
Where is the Inner Healing?
Jealousy, anger, wrong combination
Virtues not used, unnoticed
Family feud, circle of friends split
Where is the Inner Healing?
Holidays are observed

Winning-losing battle
Poverty, violence, crime circumvented
Where is the Inner Healing?
Kindness, generosity seldom practiced
Compassion, caring usually ignored
Friendliness, honesty kept aside
Where is the Inner Healing?
War, local and national currently on
Politics, controversial unstoppable
World news hoax or truth exposed
Where is the Inner Healing?
Isolation, seeking for the truth
Submission, surrender to the power
The power of healing experienced
The Inner Healing is coming near
The truth is revealed
The miracle happened
Souls enlightened
The Inner Healing is here
The Inner Healing long awaited
Transformation in the process
The power of prayer recognized
Goals: initial and ultimate achieved
The power of Inner Healing
Comes from the Almighty
The peace was felt, deep in the heart
The Inner Healing is found at last
You and me really need Inner Healing
I prayed for the Inner Healing fervently
Through GOD, His SON, and the HOLY SPIRIT
The Inner Healing we finally attained.

LORD, thank You for extending Your Healing Power! It is so clear that everyone is craving for the Inner Healing. Everyone deserves the Inner Healing. The Inner Healing must be in to every unit of the society which is the family and up to the global circumference. We should remember that the foundation of survival is the Inner Healing. It indeed aided me in my road to recovery. I witnessed the world's disaster and how the government approached the international problem. The next poem is one of the poems I did randomly, during one of my anxiety episodes. I recorded this poem continuously without interruption. Then I transcribed it on a pad paper. Whatever I recorded and wrote, were randomly spoken from my heart. This is what I witnessed.

I WITNESS FROM MY HEART

*A lot of things happened in my life, the good and the bad as well
And I thank GOD for everything, in Him I could always lean on
I know that He is always there, in my heart I could feel He guides me
every step of the way, in whatever I do, think and say
Yes, I am grateful and thankful for the great healing I received
My inner healing most of all, O LORD here I am to do Your will
To serve You, my sincere appeal, every moment of my life, every
Breath I take, I know You're there to save my soul
These LORD, I witness from my heart. You're there to listen For
every prayer I offer, You answer and grant my prayer, Wishes and
petitions for my loved ones and other people. Thank You for the gift
of intercession. I witness from my heart
Your plans for me, the prompts of the Holy Spirit
I really must depend on Thee, from my heart I speak of Your Goodness,
greatness and kindness and everything
O Holy Spirit, thank You for the gifts of poetry, for granting me a
random poem prayer, that I am taping at the moment which is now
I am going to give a title, "I Witness from My Heart".
Yes LORD from my heart it is, I witness Your awesome power,
I pray this in JESUS name, Amen!*

This random verbalization helped me in destructing my thoughts, diverting my attention and doing something constructive. The truth was, there was no rhythm in the poem and it was fluctuating with pressure. But I felt the satisfaction of verbalizing it from my heart. I said fluctuating because I was just following the flow of my thoughts, and because I was recording what I was saying without pausing, that's why there was a pressure as it continuously spoken and recorded.

And of course I expressed my deep inner thoughts, during my misery moments. I have compared the poem "I Witness From My Heart" to a fluctuating blood pressure and yet the Holy Spirit put my heart in order.

The following poem is just a short one, but very meaningful. The title is too far from spirituality, but it touches my being. Here comes the:

KALEIDOSCOPE

Life is like a kaleidoscope changes every time it moves A blink of an eye, a breath at a time
Hold on tight, grab it good
For it will roll and you must stay stood
Attitude is like a kaleidoscope,
Mood swings from unpleasant to good Everyday different faces seen
Don't shake the kaleidoscope of shame
Music is just like a kaleidoscope With different harmony and tunes
Roll it, shake it, view on it,
The sound of kaleidoscope is like An acoustic instrument
Kaleidoscope of life, attitude and music Color me, shape me and tune in with me For I am GOD's Kaleidoscope in reality
In His Image I was created, my true identity.

For the children, kaleidoscope is fun, like a telescope, like a microscope, using the magnificent eyes. But for the analogies mentioned, kaleidoscope is powerful, knowing its significance. It is true that life changes every breath it takes. That is the power beyond grasp. How we approach life, depends on attitude we show to the people or to the situations and to the world. With the harmony and blend of the music we can hear and make the life worth living. So I will climb up way up high with the kaleidoscope on my hand.

I am sure you have already read or maybe noticed the poem I placed at the first part of the book, entitled, "MYSELF." This was my first poem in this book but I wrote this at the midst of my "depersonalization" attack. I didn't even pay attention of the essence of that poem until later part of my climbing. All I know that time, I was confused, restless and didn't have any idea what was I doing. Didn't know myself neither.

As my life went on, my concept of my being self was changing. I have written poems related to myself, my image, my past and my being. So all these self-focused information were just my cane, a strong stick and strong stones on the wall that helped me in my climbing up.

Frankly speaking everything that I have shared seemed happened only yesterday. Memories are precious and should be treasured. Sometimes it felt like they were just moments ago. So MOMENTS AGO it is. Come to think of it, this poem is similar to the contents of the chapter about Psychodynamics.

MOMENTS AGO

I was young and innocent, Moments Ago
I was a little child, Moments Ago
I learned the basic education, Moments Ago
I finished the required years of academic subjects, Moments Ago
I went to college and earned a degree
Then I was ready to earn, next was job hunting,
All these were Moments Ago
I found a job, mingled around, till I met someone
Moments Ago
Many things I have accomplished
Struggles, obstacles in between success,
Happiness, sorrows and joy Moments Ago
Yes, Moments Ago, I was created in GOD's Image,
Moments Ago I said I wasn't ready
I realized that I am here in this world to prepare
Myself to meet the Almighty

*Regardless of how many years you spent
and will spend on earth, they are just,
Moments Ago.*

This was the line-up activities according to Moments Ago. The turnover of the days were so fast that's why it felt like Moments Ago. It was just a brief history of my life, young hood history.

In line with this poem is another poem, describing a woman (maybe it was me) or another certain woman. The bottom line is that woman was created in GOD's Image.

WOMAN

*I was created in GOD's Image, I am a woman
Every fiber of my being is soft and tender, I am a woman
I have the same right as any man, I am a woman
I am Me, a somebody and myself, I am a woman
The woman that I am, nobody can claim
I have my own soul, spirit and strength
I stand for my right, I don't want to fight
I just want freedom to say aloud, I am a woman
Yes, indeed I am.
In the workplace, a woman always competes
Trying hard to be assertive, aggressive and competitive
Working diligently with goals always accomplished
I am worthy of the promotion, I am a woman
In the medical field, I take care of the sick
I am a professional nurse, committed to serve
Tender, loving care, I love to render
This is me in uniform, I am a woman
Defender of justice, I see in the court
No longer for men only, but a lawyer in skirt
Women can prosecute and can give trials
Am not a lawyer, but an abiding citizen.
I am a woman
I am proud to be a woman of versatility*

A nurse, advertising lady, a mental health
Counselor, a poet, an artist and a writer
That's me the undersigned, the author
Of my life is my Creator
Thank You LORD, I am a woman.

This particular poem, "Woman" represents strongly of me. I am this woman fighting for my right, standing for what I believe in and most of all I claimed that I was created in GOD's Image. I stood for other professions. The poems above, "Moments Ago" and "Woman" helped me in developing my true Identity. When I wrote these poems I wasn't aware I should l love myself. So "Moments Ago", this "Woman" fulfilled my womanhood.

The next poem, I guessed the last poem to be included in Climbing Up Way Up High and has something to do with the process of healing. There is a time for everything. I agree that there is a time for ESTHER or THEA to climb up way up high or higher.

A TIME TO HEAL

A time to heal is a time to accept the truth
A time to heal is a time to ease the pain
A time to heal is a time to forgive
A time to heal is a time to be forgiven
Healing is a process of cleansing
Healing is a transforming process
Healing is a gift from the Holy Spirit
And healing is a peace offering
Healing leads to reconciliation
Healing results from mortification
Healing makes us stronger ever
And healing nourishes our soul
We need to pray fervently
We need to meditate profoundly
We need to spend time with our LORD
And commune with Him in His sanctuary

We need quality moments to ponder
And we need a time to heal for the awaited
Tranquility.

Part of the healing process that I went through, was I learned to forgive and I learned to ask for forgiveness. I felt light after that. There is a time to forgive and be forgiven. When it comes to the word forgive, let us remember, how many times must we forgive? Did I hear SEVEN? No, it is SEVENTY SEVEN TMES.

As the poem says, Healing is a gift from the Holy Spirit. This time, I believe that the gifts of the Holy Spirit are already there to be unwrapped by us. So, the gifts of the Holy Spirit are not only ecclesiastic because the time is anytime. Another step that I took to climb up was "the power of mortification." Our LORD JESUS experienced that. Must we, too? Anything that we worked for that comes from the heart is rewarding.

Psychological pain and the episodes of the D.A.D. challenge (Depersonalization, Anxiety and Depression) were my way of mortification. I could consider my sufferings as mortifications. I indeed offered all my aches and pains, and every afflictions to our Almighty.

I survive, I mortify, and I climb up way up high.

The Beauty of Words is spoken from the heart.

Esther Jimenez

D.A.D. CHALLENGE
(Depersonalization, Anxiety and Depression)

The Triple Mental Illness, The Battle I won, The Plight I fought.

I have three acronyms that might help us in dealing with the D.A.D. Challenge.

D-are to climb
E-xcited yet confused
P-ure heart, hungry soul
E-nlightenment, that's all it takes
R-each out, climb higher
S-elf-Analysis is healthy
O-utcome should be a positive one
N-ever give up
A-im higher…climb more
L-ove, love, love
I-dentify yourself as GOD's Image
Z-oom your goal
A-nother day is today
T-ruth will set me free
I-will be true to myself
O-ne more chance is a chance of a lifetime
N-ow or never, GOD is everywhere.

A-ngels on earth are around the corner
N-iche of a time, they arrived on time
X-anax saying good-bye

I-nspiration standing by
E-ntering the world of calmness
T-reat yourself with kindness
Y-ield to the world of oneness.

D-elight in my heart
E-nlightened by GOD
P-rofessional help is needed
R-eturn to normal succeeded
E-ngaged in positivity
S-et aside the negativity
S-teps to recovery must be followed
I-ntend to be happy, ultimate goal
O-nward and climbing up higher, thumbs up
N-ot stopping for a great reward

I hope these acronyms can help somebody in understanding how it is to be a victim of a D.A.D. (Depersonalization, Anxiety and Depression) challenge.

GOOD NEWS

Our ears loved to hear good news. Good news are always pleasing to the ears. When we hear good news we tend to shift our bad moods to good moods.

What kind of good news would you like to hear?

If you hear this good news would you be willing to share it? All the questions I just asked are worthy to talk about.

As an ordinary citizen, I am also a concerned citizen. One of the main reasons I have this book to write, "Climb Up Way Up High," is to share plainly about surviving the dreadful illness, "the depression".

I am one happy recipient of this good news.

No longer shall our countrymen be victims of "stigmatization".

On June 21, 2018, our president signed the Philippine Mental Health Law or Republic Act 11036. This Act aims to give better access to mental healthcare. And this will promote freedom to talk about mental illness. There will be free-flow conversation about the manifestation of mental illness especially *"depression"*.

As I have mentioned in the preface of my book, the *"stigma attached"* is one of the reasons victims are hesitant to reveal what they feel. The Philippine Mental Health Law also has provisions for the anti-stigma and anti-discrimination programs.

Having this new law indeed is one commendable gesture by our government officials. There is delight in my heart upon knowing that there is good news for everyone, especially for victims of depression and the family victims.

One of the main agenda that I tackle is *"stigmatization"*. Not only that I feel delight but I am relieved that I am on my way climbing up higher. I feel not only the support of my family but the support of the whole health care system. So, reaching out is easier now with this new Mental Health Law.

The victims who walk with the heads down, are now can walk with the heads up, no longer with inhibitions, but with confidence. And with this, dignity will be preserved and can live with normalcy in life.

There are more beneficial information available regarding the new law (about the mental illness). This good news is for all of us!

EPILOGUE

My journey seemed to almost reach the peak of my total recovery. While I am writing this epilogue, I feel like not wanting to end my verbalization of my story of Depression. My mind and heart seemed to have filled with more wanting to share. But an epilogue is an epilogue. All I can do is to say more about my climbing up way up high.

When I started writing this book I had an ambivalent feeling of having the desire to share and having the hesitancy to share. But I was selfless enough to let the people know that depression is definitely *treatable*; that nothing to be ashamed of and nothing to be feared of; that *"stigmatization"* is already out and known by many and that knowledge about depression is available and support is available too.

One strong measure I recommend is my own way of coping and it has proven that it works. Every time I felt depersonalized, anxious and depressed and even just bouts of stress, I let them passed by until they were gone. Sometimes they only lasted for few seconds. After letting them passed by I was taking a deep breath and was trying to shift my thoughts to something pleasant. So the span of time of the diversion process was not even ten minutes.

I have been doing this diversion shifting-technique for so long now and it was quite successful. One thing amazing is how things are connected. I didn't know that there is a phrase for the measure I was using. According to one of the information from a newsletter, it is called "cognitive distortion. So, now who ever will read this book, can use the measure I used, "cognitive distortion" technique. It's just like destructing ones thought and replacing it with pleasant ones. Reading is also very essential, especially if the information pertains to recovery.

Every story has an end, but the story of Depression never ends. It is a continuing battle between the depressed and the depression itself. So the end result of this battle remains to be seen. The most important thing is, depression is ***treatable*** even though it can recur. The nice thing is, when the recurrence appears it is easier to handle because there are measures to use to combat that depression. I know it because I have experienced it and I either ignore it or face it.

This is the paradox of a depression (a jinx and at the same time a blessing.) The irony of my mental status is, I have been a victim of an early mental illness. Children don't have enough defense mechanism to use because they are children of innocence.

I couldn't count the number of times I had anxiety attack because of my depression. The way I look at it, depression lives with me, as I live with it. My old journal book would be my witness of my dim moments. And the books I have written and the paintings I did were the outcome of my recovery and triumph. For me depression is indeed a blessing.

My life is like a rainbow, colorful because of my depersonalization, anxiety and depression. I compared my struggles, trials, pains, and challenges to the color of the rainbow. Even it seemed dim around me, the rainbow of multiplicity of obstacles gave life and reason to live.

I did a self-analysis because I was self-determined to get better and to guide me in avoiding self-destruction and to know more of myself, that I should love myself first, so I can give a true love with sincerity.

There are three strong foundations that pushed me to climb up higher and I considered it a success. (1) the strong support of my family and friends (2) the compliance I went through of the available resources as to the medical and psychiatric aspects (3) the fervent prayers and our Almighty's answer to the prayers.

The D.A.D. (Depersonalization, Anxiety and Depression) challenges are still around, but with Our GOD Almighty's help I will survive. I will continue **to climb up way up high.**

As the title says, Climb Up Way Up High is a process of surviving a struggle. It is an analogy of how a person struggles, suffers, and survives the dreadful illness called depression.

This book is about getting away from the stigma attached and developing confidence that depression is treatable.

This is a confession made by the author of her dim moments, her long years of suffering and yet found herself "climbing up, way up high" to search for the inner healing.

With the support of her family, the compliance of the author's psychiatric regimen, and the utmost fervent prayers, the climbing she did was a success. It would be a great relief to have this *stigmatization* be in oblivion.

CLIMB UP WAY UP HIGH

CPSIA information can be obtained
at www.ICGtesting.com
Printed in the USA
FSHW021906310520
70451FS